Awakened by Death

AWAKENED BY DEATH

LIFE-GIVING LESSONS FROM THE MYSTICS

CHRISTIANA N. PETERSON

BROADLEAF BOOKS
MINNEAPOLIS

AWAKENED BY DEATH
Life-Giving Lessons from the Mystics

Cover design and illustration by James Kegley

Print ISBN: 978-1-5064-6116-8
eBook ISBN: 978-1-5064-6117-5

To Mom, for giving me life
and so much love
To Matthew: 'til death do us part

WHERE O DEATH

this breath
the preacher said
was like God

no eye has seen
it force
the wintered stalks
to bend and nod

they remain
blandly colored
these unplanted muted
but surely rooted
stalks

sounding together
as a crowd clapping
or lapping
of the sea

not standing guard
but still guarding
the edge
where ordinary
tips into grief

where shadows of dormant trees
square off the grass beds
where arthritic fingers
linger over
the place of the dead

how ominous it should feel
inside the four-square
on the bench
from the sisters of the shadows
there

But only sad

the skeletal remains
of a wind chime
adorning a headstone

don't ring

only there is the sound
of those stalks
applauding our efforts
at soothing

the sting*

*Christiana Peterson, "Where O Death," *The Curator*, September 26, 2013, https://tinyurl.com/sulkaop.

Contents

INTRODUCTION: GRAVEYARD MEDITATIONS

I love walking in cemeteries. A few years ago, I was living with my family in an intentional community on a 180-acre farm in Illinois. On the edge of the woods, at the highest point of the community, was a cemetery that served as the final resting place for members of our community and for people connected to our community who struggled to afford a typical American funeral. At the lowest point was a second cemetery—a small plot across from the cow pasture by the creek. Children and babies were buried there.

I walked more often to the smaller cemetery, sometimes with my own children. We would stop there just before we climbed Stagecoach Pass to pick fruit on Blueberry Hill. We sat on the mossy bench that tilted into the wet earth and noticed the rusty trinkets and charms that hadn't been shined, the grass that hadn't been cut. I didn't know any of the families whose babies were buried there. They had moved away long ago. A tree had fallen into a patch of daffodils; these bold yellow blossoms were usually the first sign that spring would be emerging soon.

Sometimes I wondered if nature itself respected the grief that must've surrounded the deaths of these babies.

There was always a stillness in that place, as if the wind kept vigil over the gravestones. The quiet was only occasionally broken by the sounds of passing cars, mooing cattle, or a creek that drifted or roared, depending on how much rain had fallen that week.

When my children and I sat on the bench sinking into the mud, we noticed the tiny span of dates, the marking of very short lives. We talked about death. We said a prayer. I didn't always know what to say in the shadow of such grief. My daughter Neva took everything in as she usually did: observantly, waiting to say more later.

After we picked our berries, we often walked past the small cemetery again on our way home. "Maybe I will be buried there when I die," Neva once said, simply.

At six years old, Neva seemed to have already learned a lesson I'd been trying to learn my whole life. Maybe she was better equipped with the imaginative capacity to hold the complex tensions of life with the knowledge of death.

***

When I lived in Scotland during graduate school, nearly twenty years ago, there were two more cemeteries that I loved. I walked the same trail every day, a path that ran parallel to a creek and intersected with trees whose roots looked as ancient and otherworldly as Middle-earth. At the end of the walk, when I felt I could go no further, the path crossed a road at the edge of town. Between a break in the low stone wall there was an old cemetery. As I approached, rabbits who burrowed around the headstones would leap out between them, stirred by a visitor in the late morning light.

At another place along the same path, the aptly named Hallow Hill rose gently above a cottage where an old water wheel still turned. Atop the hill were traces of a Pictish cemetery from the fifth through ninth centuries, the remains of a people who lived in Scotland in Roman times. The graves were so old that I couldn't fathom their age. Still, I spent some moments trying to imagine what life was like for the Picts and those who inhabited these hills and forests long ago.

***

Cemeteries that have gone a little wild are my favorite kind, those that have been left to the weeds or whose headstones are aged by a time far away. The wildest cemeteries remind us that we will all return to the earth. The headstones themselves will last far longer than those whose graves they mark.

But I am also drawn to cemeteries because of a lifelong fixation on death. An early awareness of death is embedded in my family history. My paternal grandfather died when my father was only fourteen years old, so my grandmother raised my father on her own. Familial and cultural pressures demanded that she throw her grief into boxes of folded and dusty memories, locking them away for us, her grandchildren, to find after she died. Death formed their mother-son relationship, and it shaped my father. It shaped the way he walked, the tilt of his head, his warm kisses, his exorbitant generosity, and also the secret parts of his heart that I think he never recognized.

My father, with his death-formed view of the world, shaped me too.

Even as a child, I would lie in bed and wonder what it would feel like to die. When I began having children, death reached out to me in new ways, ways that frightened me and shook my foundations. I first began to write the sketches of this book in those difficult years when parenting welcomed me into a kind of love that brings both infinite joy and the potential for the greatest pain I could imagine.

My ability to make a path through different cemeteries is, perhaps, one of many privileges I've had in life. Not only have I been able to live in many places but my life hasn't been marked by violence and war. It hasn't been marked by the death of a child or the traumatic death of a loved one.

Still, I have experienced deaths of various kinds, and I have lived through the deaths of people I love. This doesn't make me more or less qualified to write about death than anyone else. In some sense, each of us is an authority on death. Death is in all of our histories, whether we lost a loved one early in our lives, we have faced life-threatening illnesses, or it's just a lingering part of our cultural narratives.

As mystic Howard Thurman says, every human is "involved in the endless cycle of birth, of living and dying," and therefore expertly qualified to be "a key interpreter of the meaning of the totality of the experience."[1] We are all qualified to talk about death because we will all die.

But just because we are all qualified doesn't mean we will actually choose to face death before it happens. I wanted to write this book to uncover the way the fear of death shows up in my own life but also to explore how it shows up in our wider culture. Many of us construct our lives in order to avoid talking about or even thinking about death. This is, of course, understandable and, in many ways, a natural response to the desire to survive. Death is the most complex and mysterious of human experiences, and we are embedded in a culture that has misplaced the language and rituals to talk about such things. Our death fears often show up in our lives in ways we aren't conscious of.

The mystics in the history of the church can help. Maybe it was their tenderness to the wrenching parts of the human experience that equipped them to encounter God in visions and mystical experiences. Many of them were marked by suffering and death.

In the second-century church, mystical theology was a study of Scripture that sought to encounter God with the whole self. Seventeenth-century mystic Madame Guyon speaks of this mystical approach to reading the Bible: "If you read quickly . . . you will be like a bee that merely skims the surface of a flower. Instead . . . you must become as the bee that penetrates into the depths of the flower. You plunge deeply within to remove its deepest nectar."[2] Reading Scripture was more than just a rational endeavor; it involved both a deep contemplative spirit and a life of action.

If you search the word *mysticism* on the internet, you come up with a range of images: occult symbols, mandalas, ethereal beings in yoga poses, depictions of ancient mystics, and even creatures with wings. The world of mysticism can be colorful and vibrant. But these images are an indication of both a cultural confusion about mysticism and its definitions and understandings changing over time.

Mysticism is a relatively new term in the big scheme of the mystical life of faith. It was first used in the 1700s by stodgy Enlightenment thinkers who were critical of "religious enthusiasm."[3] Scholar Joy Bostic says that a lot of this criticism was directed more particularly at female spiritual expression. *Mysticism*, at first, was a derogatory term for "public demonstrations of ecstatic religion as being outside the institutional norms of Christianity."[4] It wasn't until the nineteenth century that the word *mysticism* began to denote something a little more positive: a "loosely spiritual, emancipatory, universal, heterogeneous religious path."[5] Yet during the New Age movement of the twentieth century, the academic world was rather snobby about mysticism; it was beneath their scholarly dignity.[6]

Scholars are more interested in mysticism now, and some religious institutions are trying to reconnect with their mystical roots. After all, every religion has had its mystics, though mystics themselves are difficult to categorize. Their experiences and lives are as numerous as they are, but most of them had life-altering encounters with God. Evelyn Underhill, one of the foremost writers on mysticism in the early twentieth century, laid out the stages in the mystical life like this: "awakening, purification [purgation], illumination, voices and visions, contemplation and introversion, ecstasy and rapture, the dark night of the soul and union with the divine."[7]

In other words: great mystics are born into a certain way of life, a way of life that begins to feel ill fitting. Many have visions or unusual encounters with God or Jesus or the divine, what Underhill might call ecstasies, visions, or prophecies. They often have deeply painful encounters too. Depending on their culture or definitions, these painful or terrifying encounters have been called demons or even Satan. Encounters with their own brokenness, their own inner lack, could be called purification, purgation, or later on, the dark night of the soul.

At the end of this darkness, in illumination, mystics encounter a deep awareness that God has rescued them from their brokenness and, despite their human frailty, has enveloped them in a desperate, deep, and intimate love. This awareness of God's love seems to be the catalyst for transformation. In fact, Howard Thurman wrote that mystical encounters were only truly "authentic" if they produced the fruit of "active engagement in community."[8]

By this definition, very few of us are mystics. And yet, every time I've spoken about the mystics, someone has approached me afterward to tell me that they have had mystical encounters—experiences that feel unexplainable—that they've shared with few people for fear of being labeled as crazy. When they read the mystics, they feel like they aren't alone anymore.

Many people are having mystical encounters with God. We may not be like some of the ancient mystics, having visions or encounters or ecstasies, but all of us can live toward a mystical faith, a faith that longs for union with God and rests in the mystery of God. All Christians are called to this mystical life of faith, one that produces the good fruit Thurman speaks of. Author and mysticism scholar Michael Cox goes so far as to say that Christianity itself is a "fundamentally mystical religion."[9]

The Old Testament is full of mystical writing and imagery. Some of the biblical writers of the New Testament, like the apostle Paul and John the Evangelist, experienced transformative divine encounters with God.

The story of God and God's creatures from the beginning of creation is one of mystical union. Creation in Genesis emerges from the relational unity of the Trinity, of three persons who experience community with one another. This triune God imbues creation, and particularly humans, with *imago Dei*, the image of God. The beginning of the story of Eden, of a paradise garden of plenty, is a story of creatures who are wholly unified with God, whose DNA is God's. Humans' separation from God feels exceptionally devastating when seen through the eyes of this original mystical union.

The post-Eden narrative is one of God ever moving toward union with humans again and finally making it possible for full unity by indwelling, incarnating God's self into human flesh. One of the foundational beauties of the Christian story is that, through the person of Jesus and the Holy Spirit, we have the "capacity for intimate fellowship with God."[10]

The Christian mystics, with their posture of humility and openness to God, can open our eyes to our own spiritual capacities. They show us that the "spiritual sense is latent in us all" and that we can begin to imagine and conceive of the truth that being unified with God is possible.[11]

The goal of the mystical life is, ultimately, total union with God. But a mystical life of faith is never done in isolation. Even the mystics of the church who were hermits were informed by the community of faith, by reading

Scripture, and by experiencing God in the rest of creation. The move toward unity with God, even (or especially!) with people so pious, is often somewhat odd. Mystics are rather peculiar, doing unconventional things in order to seek the God that comforted them in stunning visions. Some of them, like Saint Francis of Assisi, gave all their possessions away. Like Catherine of Siena, they sought extreme solitude with God. Some died for their faith.

These odd, wonderful, and very human figures of the church have captured me as I look at death. A clear-eyed view of death often comes from living a mystical life. In a culture that is structured to avoid thoughts of mortality, facing our fear of death goes against the grain. If we are willing to push against the status quo, the mystics can guide us, not because they are perfect but because they have been there. They understand what it means to stare down a culture that fears death with a frenzy.

The mystics have given me permission to lean into death. They have given me some language to speak to the mystery. To lament. To grieve. To turn my heart to God even when I am afraid or I don't understand.

***

When I first began to write this book, I optimistically outlined it chronologically, planning to write a whole history of death using the lens of the mystics. What began as an enthusiastic trip through history, however, became an increasingly dark and murky traverse through a landscape that, after a while, I couldn't define. It wasn't that I was "stuck in the weeds." It was more like I'd pushed through a veil into a nefarious labyrinth that seemed intent on having me die in there.

I reached a moment of desperation when I received an eagerly anticipated copy of a seven-hundred-page academic tome called *The Work of the Dead* by Thomas W. Laqueur. On the fifth page of the preface, Laqueur says that after decades of research, he finally had to accept that he could *not* write a history of death. It simply wasn't possible.

I felt gutted. If this scholar had abandoned such a prospect after decades of research, how could I attempt it? Laqueur knew that there was no clear historical through line about how different cultures (or even one single culture) die, respond to death, grieve death, practice death rituals, bury their dead, or treat their dying. There are certainly patterns attached to historical periods, but naming them necessarily requires some measure of oversimplification. Historical periods are not about just one thing or another. Though we are firmly rooted in our time and place, we are also complex creatures who respond to the world according to our internal ways of seeing and being.

Researching death and religion has taken me to some dark places. I've been discouraged by the enormity of my writing task, and I've also beheld through my research the horrible things we humans have done to one another. I spent weeks researching the slave ships that decimated populations in Africa, feeling sick as I tried to visualize the measurements of the spaces that held enslaved people, the tiny spaces in slave ships that became their coffins. I read history books by indigenous authors who wanted to reclaim the narratives of their people. I read about how Columbus and other explorers—bolstered by a spirit of exploration from their European kingdoms —possessed, killed, raped, and stole from Native peoples. And I struggled with how to write about all of this death.

Here is where I landed: Laqueur was right. One person cannot write the history of death. One person cannot capture all there is to say about this most complex human experience. So I haven't tried to do that. Instead, I've tried to give a historical sketch of approaches to death in the Western world using the lives of the mystics as an anchor.

I've given you some of their stories. Stories of those within a complicated history who stood out and offered spiritual wisdom to their culture's approach to loss, terror, fear, and death. I drew toward the wisdom of those mystics who captured my imagination during times of emotional turmoil and who have since been fellow pilgrims on my journey of faith. Their perceptive and unflinching look at their own internal darkness allowed them to approach the darkness of the world with eyes that were always searching for God.

I've also offered a part of myself, sketches of my own story of deaths, little and large, and the landscape of my fears, challenges, and hopes. I offer them with trepidation and trembling, hoping that you will resonate with my particular take on this human journey that we all must walk.

***

I live in Ohio now, and when I take my walks to our local cemetery, I often make it to the top of the hill at dusk, in time to see the sun lowering behind the tall trees. Some of the dates on the stone grave markers are nearly rubbed away. Still, they are not so old as the Pictish graves on my walks in Scotland. I look out across the plots and see, for a moment, how many lives they encompass, how much human pain and joy is buried in this soil.

When I took a stroll with Neva one afternoon, I asked her if she wanted to go to the cemetery. "Not really," she said. She was now ten and more aware of the realities of life and death than she had been at six. In the years since we sat at the cemetery beside Stagecoach Pass, she's sat in another cemetery to bury someone we all loved.

"Do you know why I like to walk in the cemetery?" I said.

"Because you love death."

We both laughed.

"No," I said. "It's because I'm actually afraid of death. I'm trying to look at it head-on. And going to the cemetery helps me do that."

Although I've always thought the word *graveyard* sounds more ancient and romantic, the origin of the word *cemetery* is much older. *Cemetery* comes from the Greek word for "dormitory" or "sleeping place." Ancient Greeks would often bury the bodies of their family members in their own homes. Scholars believe this tradition is from a ninth-century decree stating that it was good for youths to have the dead buried within their communities so they could learn to stand such "spectacles" and look upon dead bodies without fear.[12]

It wasn't until the eighth century that Saint Cuthbert got permission to put burial grounds near churches. The church came to view burial grounds as sacred and buried the dead as close to churches as possible, sometimes even within the walls.[13]

Modern cemeteries are now larger burial places that

aren't attached to churches. They are city-owned acreages or private memorial gardens that are often far outside the city walls so that our youth don't see such spectacles.

I was never particularly interested in seeking out the dark for its own sake. In fact, I was always trying to push it out of my vision. But life and loss have changed me. I have started to seek out the spectacle, to welcome the quiet darkness of twilight, to face the fear of death.

When I walk in a cemetery or graveyard, there are times when I feel a deep peace, a knowledge that one day, I will also follow the cycle of life and death. Sometimes I picture what my gravestone will look like. At other times, I am afraid about what will come at the moment of death, terrified that all I have put my faith and hope in is ridiculous and I will simply cease to exist.

These feelings are all normal. Graveyards and cemeteries are places of meditation, places of contemplation. They are ripe with a silence that has a trajectory, a focus. They are full of a quiet knowing.

Sister Theresa Aletheia Noble, who writes a series of memento mori Lenten devotions, keeps a ceramic skull on her desk so that she might face her fear and remember her death. Maybe daily graveyard meditations are my ceramic skull; they are a way toward memento mori, a Latin phrase that means "remember that you will die."

While most people in our culture don't think about death that much, the terror weaves its way into the ways we structure our lives. What I told Neva that day is right: I am trying to look at what I fear. This book is also my memento mori, my way of approaching that fear, of remembering my death.

But it is an offering, too, an encouragement, an urging

to you, my readers. I hope you will be willing to walk the paths with me up toward Blueberry Hill and we may sit together on the tilted bench. Let's take a walk and enjoy the sweat that rolls down our necks as we enjoy glimpses of rabbits that scatter between the headstones.

Shall we be brave and take on the unfathomable contemplation of our death? Shall we look at death with the eyes of the very young? Shall we examine our lives the way Madame Guyon taught us to read the Bible, diving deeply within "to remove its deepest nectar"? Maybe we can recapture our imaginative capacities and lean into the discomfort that comes when we peel our eyes away from distractions. Maybe we can allow ourselves to feel the somewhat painful tingling that begins when our sleeping selves wake up.

Let us wake up together. Let us wake up so that we may face our inevitable falling asleep. Let us wake up so that we can remember our death.

When you come past my grave
And I am dead and rotten,
Just hold your nose
And keep on trottin'.
—L. Morrison, ed., *A Diller a Dollar**

Six feet of earth make all men of one size.
—Old American proverb

The last enemy to be destroyed is death.
—1 Corinthians 15:26

*Iserson, 576.

PART I

THE BODY TURNED INSIDE OUT: THE MEDIEVAL MYSTICS

1

THE GREAT LEVELER

A few years ago, my husband and I moved to a small town in Ohio. We bought an old house on a quaint street that turned out to be the town locus for trick-or-treating. Most of the excitement on Halloween night, when children begin knocking on our door at 5:30 p.m. in an endless stream, is focused on a house just down the street from us.

The owners of that house—a large, old stone building with arches and a front garden fenced in by a short white gate—begin to decorate for Halloween in stages. Skulls appear first, adorning the roof and front gables. Then the skeletons emerge, appearing to dance across the front garden. Life-size figures materialize next, gray hoods and cloaks tattered at the edges, swaying in the wind. Eerie orange lights, strung up across the white fence, illuminate the night.

Finally, on Halloween night, the inhabitants of the house disguise themselves in full-length costumes: they are werewolves, witches, or even Death with his scythe and ragged cloak. They stand imposingly in the garden behind the white gate. Prospective trick-or-treaters must pass by these figures, talk to them even, before they get to the nice ladies in their purple parkas handing out candy at the front door.

Our first Halloween in the neighborhood, our four-year-old daughter Annalee wouldn't go near the figures, not even for a handful of candy. But an hour later, Annalee came bursting through the front door with something to tell me: she'd marched right up to those masked figures, shook one of their hands, and collected her candy. Though she wouldn't have been able to articulate it yet, she was exhilarated by facing down her fears.

In many ways, Halloween is an appropriate time and place for many of us to face our fears. At various times in the history of the celebration, Halloween has come to represent the thin veil between worlds, between the fairy and the human world, between life and death, between the rich and the poor.

The history of Halloween and the images and traditions that are associated with it hark back to some of the more harrowing events in Western history. Theological understandings that have emerged out of cultural crises have become lodged in a collective memory in ways we might not even realize. The messages we've received from our culture about death, the afterlife, and our ability to escape death have been and continue to be shaped by this history. Taking a look at some of the death practices, art, and rituals from the medieval period might illuminate our own views of death and make us more aware of the ways we push death to the recesses of our imaginations. It might make us look at Halloween a little differently too.

***

On the horizon, a dozen ships swayed on the Black Sea as they headed toward the docks. Since trade routes had opened up between Italian city-states and other cities around the Black Sea and the Mediterranean, the Port of Messina in Sicily was always a bustle of activity. From the perspective of the ships, people meandering and swarming on the docks probably resembled the scattering of rats. It was a new era of trade and expansion.

But if a large sailing vessel could behave strangely, these dozen ships were certainly doing so.

As they drew nearer to the coast, their course seemed to waver even more than the rolling of the sea would naturally allow. To the educated observer, they seemed not only unmoored but unmanned. When the locals timidly boarded the strange ships, hoping to discover goods and wares from trade voyages, what they found instead made even the skeptics cross themselves in fear.

They were ghost ships, full of dead men.

Boats like this would start arriving at ports all over Europe and North Africa in the coming months of 1347 and 1348, ships carrying sailors from Kaffa in Crimea who had managed to escape sieges where soldiers were dying as much from illness as from war. All of them carried a sickness that had already devastated much of Asia, accelerating an end to the Mongol rule over China.

Not all of the twelve ghost ships' sailors were dead, but the few who were alive and had managed to stumble onto the gangplank were covered in the veneer of death. The Italians sent the ships back out to sea for quarantine, but the rats and their fleas didn't notice. The fleas piled hungrily out into the sea of people at the port, mixing right in with the swarm of the city. The Black Death sank its teeth into Europe and sucked the vitality from it. This catastrophic disease spread uncontrollably and not only culled the population of Europe by 30–50 percent[1] but devastated the whole world.

***

Many cities in Europe were economically destroyed by the Black Death. Construction on cathedrals stopped because workers were dying in such large numbers; artists died, and developing schools of education had to be abandoned.[2] As with every other century in human history, a natural preoccupation and fear of death touched the people of the medieval world. As Phoebe S. Spinrad notes in her book *The Summons of Death on the Medieval and Renaissance English Stage*, "The death rate of the human race has always been one hundred percent, and few societies have failed to notice the fact."[3] But the swiftness and totality of the casualties during the Black Death compounded this fear.

Even before the Black Death, life during the Middle Ages was hard, and any number of things could cut it short: illnesses and accidents we consider relatively minor in our modern Western society, rancid food, wounds that turned gangrenous. But on top of that, and most anxiety producing, was another dread. In medieval

Europe, the fear of death was ultimately a fear of the afterlife—especially a terror of the burning pits of hell.[4]

While it's true that ideas of the last judgment, heaven, and hell certainly emerged from specific readings of biblical texts, many imaginative and theological articulations of this afterlife grew from other sources during the Middle Ages. Dante Alighieri's *Divine Comedy*, an influential literary masterpiece of the early fourteenth century, was completed just over two decades before the beginning of the Black Death. While Dante didn't create a theology of the afterlife, with his genius he crafted a work of art so effective that it still influences the creative imaginations of many Christians, even if they don't know it. His nine circles of hell, each with increasingly creative and torturous torments, are particularly potent in the imagination.[5]

The effects of the Black Death and life in medieval times showed up in many art forms like *The Divine Comedy*, including visual, literary, and even artistic physical movement. When religious leaders wanted an alternative to the bawdy dances of their parishioners, they choreographed an ecclesiastical dance in which a personified Death came for persons from every section of society—the rich and poor alike—and danced them to their graves. The *Danse Macabre* or Dance of Death became a way of coping with what must have felt like apocalyptic devastation in the years after the Black Death. Eventually this death dance was portrayed in visual art and written poetry, the most famous being a mural at the cemetery of the Holy Innocents in Paris. For anyone who saw, read, or participated in the *Danse Macabre*, the resounding message was that death was the great "social-leveler": the rich were as powerless before the inevitability of death as the farmer, the midwife, and the king.[6]

The *Danse Macabre* was one of the ways that people of the time practiced memento mori (remembering death/mortality). Some say the origins of the phrase *memento mori* go all the way back to ancient Rome when lower-ranking officials would whisper the phrase to generals returning from the victories of battle, to encourage humility. There are myths about Trappist monks in medieval times whispering "memento mori" to one another in their hallways (Trappist monks deny this).[7] Still, many religious traditions and cultures have found it necessary to remember the inevitability of death. Whether they use the phrase or not, the grave art of the medieval period, the *Danse Macabre*, visual images of skulls, and daily prayers for the dead by some religious orders are all ways that people have connected to their mortality.

The visual depictions of death itself were varied in the Middle Ages. Some depicted death as another aspect of one's own self. Sometimes death was an unbeatable horseman of the apocalypse, mowing down those in his way. Or maybe death was the hooded figure, much like those hooded figures hanging from the house down my street at Halloween: ragged cloak, skeletal face, a scythe in hand.

It's no wonder that so many depictions of death existed. When the psyche becomes overrun "with chaos or destruction on too vast a scale to be absorbed," Spinrad says, "the natural impulse is to make the concept more familiar so that it can be dealt with."[8] Medieval people managed their death fears with the only tools they had. And many times, these dances and depictions, both literary and visual, were created to encourage viewers and readers to remember that they would die and to repent before it was too late.

In the *Danse Macabre*, kings, princes, paupers, and maids would all end in death, equally. Clergy were no exception. Priests and bishops perished along with everyone else, leaving the dying laymen and women without religious authorities to perform their death rituals. This further intensified the terror of death. If you didn't have clergy to send you off to the afterlife, would you automatically end up in those burning circles of hell?

To soothe the minds of the fearful, religious texts called ars moriendi (the art of dying) began to pop up. Ars moriendi offered spiritual and religious meditations, prayers, and rites for lay people who didn't have access to a priest at death so they could repent and have their souls entrusted to God.[9] These religious texts taught parishioners how to die well and provided comfort for those who believed they had lived godly lives worthy of heaven. For others, the texts served to fend off the horrors of that eternal burning lake of fire.[10]

The world of the Middle Ages has always been fascinating to those of us who are interested in death. Religious responses like ars moriendi and the changes in art reveal the way a culture responds to the swiftness of death on an apocalyptic scale. The Middle Ages are a petri dish for human responses to chaos.

Most of us in the Western world are not accustomed to the disruption of our normal lives. Our responses to such disruptions, both on an individual scale and on a societal level, might reveal our psychologies. How would we respond if our cities were permanently altered? If our architecture and schools and churches no longer looked the same. What would these disruptions do to our thoughts about death?

***

Three miles from where I lived in St. Andrews, Scotland, during graduate school, there is a small country stone church, surrounded by a graveyard. The church itself dates back to the nineteenth century, relatively young for the buildings in that part of the world. An old cross is evidence that the graveyard might have been the site of another place of worship, thousands of years old.

Though the church is picturesque, it isn't the main draw for many visitors. The church is just the entry point for another more ancient site. To reach this unique place, my friends and I walked down a dirt path behind the church's graveyard. We passed a seemingly ordinary stone that was carved by the Picts in about 800 A.D., the same group whose graves were at the top of Hallow Hill on my cemetery walk. This stone stood guard at the entrance to the forest path. Along the path, we discovered a well filled with a few inches of murky water, leaves, and disparate coin offerings from eager visitors. Beside it was a narrow and steep set of stone steps. They were mossy and worn, so we took our time descending, bracing our hands on the rock to keep from slipping. As we descended, our fingers brushed against carvings hewn from the stone: the face of an old man, Celtic knots, a Celtic cross of unknown age.

When the path opened out into a clearing and a bubbling stream, we saw strange pieces of color hanging from trees, strung across the rocks. These bits and bobs, vibrant tokens, and ribbons were from visitors who had journeyed to the ancient pagan site.

Mystery surrounds the origins of this place called Dunino Den. It was likely used as a worship site for the ancient Celts that occupied this land. When I planned my visit, I wasn't sure what to expect. Local Scottish friends had encouraged me to explore the site, and it turned out to be a highlight of my time in Scotland, something I will always remember. But I have to admit that I felt something else in Dunino Den, and it wasn't altogether pleasant: a shiver on the skin, a brush of something unseen, a cold wind breathing down my neck.

Dunino is a place that, like Halloween, marries the pre-Christian and Christian cultures of ancient times. It's a place where pagan gods became Christian saints and worship sites were consecrated for the church.

According to academic folklorist Jack Santino, many of the customs we have at Halloween have their origins in the Celtic celebration of Samhain, "the first day of the New Year in the Celtic calendar." The Celts were an ancient people whose descendants would become the Irish, Scottish, and Welsh, with some living in parts of northern France. Because Samhain was a day of transition in the Celtic calendar when the harvest was ended and winter would bring darkness, it directed attention to the veils between the seasons and between worlds: the human and fairy world, the world of the living and the world of the dead. The tradition of going door-to-door bringing or begging food was associated with the appeasing of spirits, who were often portrayed by revelers in masks.

When early Christian missionaries arrived in Ireland before the fifth century, they attempted to understand this culture's sacred practices and instead of rejecting them outright, consecrated them for Christ.[11] In an effort to appeal to Celtic peoples, missionaries attached Christian holidays to the season of Samhain. Established on November 1, All Saints' Day, or All Hallows' Day (*hallow* means holy), was and is a day on the liturgical calendar to honor the saints, especially those who didn't have a particular feast day already. But the effort to engage the traditions of this particular group (without obliterating them) meant that some of the traditions and beliefs still lingered in the consciousness and memory of the Celtic people.

This is clear in a place like Dunino Den, where pilgrims and visitors flock, even centuries later, and leave their offerings. The Celtic ideas of this veil between worlds and "the traveling dead" were so powerful that totally eradicating them was impossible. Instead of eliminating these traditions, the church adopted November 2 as All Souls' Day, a day for the living to pray for the dead.[12]

All Saints' Day and All Souls' Day eventually became permanent parts of the liturgical season in the Roman Catholic Church. All Hallows' Eve, the night *before* All Saints' Day, became what we know as Halloween, that day when the veil between worlds was slight and people interacted with spirits through feasting.

Many cultures besides the Celts have experienced a blending of traditional celebrations and church holidays around this time of year. The Mexican tradition known as el Día de los Muertos, or the Day of the Dead, has become a festival-like series of days in early November. The Day of the Dead is a time when festivalgoers commune with the dead through feasting. The occasion is both serious and celebratory.[13] Mass is observed in Mexico during this time, but it mingles with "folk celebrations" like placing food and artistic creations on the graves of your loved ones or parading elaborate and colorful calavera skulls throughout the streets.[14]

Many times throughout Mexico's history, political and religious powers attempted to tamp down the Day of Dead celebrations because they found them threatening. Historian Juan Pedro Viqueira argues that these nightly visits to cemeteries, visits made by men, women, and children, horrified those with wealth and power who "looked to expel death from social life."[15] Day of the Dead celebrations and traditions reminded those who had the most to lose from death that they would still die. Like everyone else.

Just as the *Danse Macabre* reminded medieval Europe of the great social-leveling power of death, so did (and does) the Day of the Dead remind the people of Mexico that, no matter who they were, they were going to die.

Though it's likely the only time of year that we, as a culture, engage with death, a typical Halloween in America sometimes looks more like a child's holiday than a way to think about our mortality. Still, there might actually be some important things happening underneath the surface of our Halloween traditions.

When my family and I lived and worked on a farm in Illinois, our community celebrated a harvest festival in October. We played games in the meadow, ate good food, and relished being outdoors in the last days before winter. Even though the largest part of the harvesting was over, it was our communal way of celebrating the gifts that the earth and our work had yielded during the year. I didn't understand as a child growing up in the city, with so much ready access to food, that our lives are dependent upon farmers and their understanding of the seasons and the weather.

During Halloween, those boundaries between urban and rural life are crossed, if only momentarily: urbanites often visit farms to pick out pumpkins or gourds and make creative displays of vegetables that outfit their porches and mantles. Because most city dwellers are so far removed from the way their food is cultivated, grown, harvested, and raised, it's a connection, however small, to the things that nourish us and give us life. It's also a reminder of the seasonal approach of the earth's death or dormancy. The time surrounding Halloween is a celebration of the life and harvest that nourished us throughout year. As winter approaches, we steel ourselves for the scarcity that will come.

For those of us who decorate our homes and send our costumed children out to walk the streets of our communities, Halloween becomes something that emerges out of our domestic lives. If we don't know what it's like to feel threatened by violence, homelessness, or poverty, Halloween can be a time of accepting, if briefly, that death will ultimately be the only *sure* threat to this safe refuge we call home. Through the symbols, costumes, vegetables, and skeletons, "death takes its place as a part of life, a natural part of everyday life."[16]

And what of the displays of skeletons that frightened my daughter on our first Halloween in Ohio? Children know from a young age that skulls and skeletons represent something scary and taboo. Even if they can't grasp the significance, they sense the fear that surrounds these things.

One evening, a week before our most recent Halloween, Annalee asked if we could visit the Halloween house. We bundled up in our coats and I held her hand as we walked down the block. We stood across the street for a moment. She noticed the plastic graves popping out of the front yard and the robed skeleton that loomed larger than me.

"Do you want to cross the street and look closer?" I asked. For a few moments, she refused. Then I saw a tiny nod of her head.

She was quiet while we stood in front of the Halloween house, which gruesomely and stridently proclaimed the reality of death. But she stood resolutely, then pointed to a smaller skeleton, contorted in a humorous way as it climbed up a light fixture. She started to laugh. And then she was ready to go back home.

Reminding ourselves that we are only skeletons on the inside is something we have to do again and again. I have appreciated the liturgical calendar's insistence that death must be remembered, every year. Many churches continue to celebrate All Saints' and All Souls' Days. Having a few holidays that force us into the rhythm is a good thing. Celebrations like Halloween or Day of the Dead can be ways for a culture to face the fact that power, wealth, comfort, and security will not save us from the inevitability of death.

Still, it is understandable if Halloween or such holidays send a shiver down your spine the way Dunino Den did for me. If our collective memories of the Black Death are any indication, some of us are more sensitive to the veil between worlds. Maybe those sensitivities are a warning, a reminder that it's important to put death in its place, to not engage in activities that will overcome us with fear.

Sometimes situations beyond our control will force us to reckon with our mortality. But I suspect we will always need some traditions to help us remember our death year after year and those who have gone before us. We also need a chance to laugh at those silly dancing skeletons.

In our Illinois community, a month or so after our harvest festival, we would gather in the evening of November 1, the traditional date of All Saints' Day, and have a "Lantern Festival." We ate cookies and drank hot chocolate and talked about the many spiritual meanings of light and darkness. We constructed a bonfire and walked the community grounds in the night, holding lanterns in our gloved hands, our breath misting in the cold as we sang hymns and songs about light and loss. Then we collected sticks and stood in a circle, tossing them one by one into the fire, speaking the names of those we'd loved and lost in the past year.

It was our little way of feasting with the dead, an evening to remember that we are just the sum of the parts we can't see. Just like everyone else, we, too, will one day be a bag of bones.

2

THE SPECTER OF AGE

I find myself meandering through pharmacy aisles sometimes, looking for affordable eye cream while my toddler squirms in the grocery cart. Wrinkles and lines are deepening across my forty-two-year-old forehead and eyes. I haven't been able to bring myself to spend $17.95 on half an ounce of antiaging eye cream, even though I'm curious to see if it will work. Instead, I choose the cheapest night cream, with its enticing promise of agelessness, and drop it into my basket.

Like many of us, I want to take care of my health and my skin. If I am totally honest, though, the allure of the night cream's greater promises tugs at a longing and fear deep inside me.

In 2017 global cosmetic products were worth $445 billion, and their value only continues to grow.[1] Despite the booming industry, my mother, who has just reached her seventies, feels that very little in fashion and beauty caters to women her age. Though the narrative of female empowerment has more recently become good for business, the language of "'tackle' and 'beat' blemishes or 'defy' aging" has been replaced with less aggressive words to smooth over the wrinkles of patriarchy.[2] *Renew* and *revitalize* sound more like female empowerment and appeal to our desire for basic self-care needs.[3] The verbs might've changed, but they are the same products aimed at the same problems.

It's difficult to resist being caught up in the appeal of these products. I am in the confusing position of being aware of these marketing ploys, yet still longing for the youth and vitality these products assure me are within reach. The underlying messaging of the beauty industry is subtle but potent, and I am simultaneously repulsed by this message and pulled into its perfumed embrace: there is something fundamentally wrong with me. "No matter how low you turn the volume," Chelsea Summers says in an essay called "Aging Ghosts in the Skincare Machine," "the specter of aging wails, open-mouthed and horrified, at the core of skincare."[4]

"Open-mouthed and horrified" might be hyperbole, or maybe it captures more viscerally what I and many others are feeling. Anxiety about aging can manifest in various ways, but one thing many people do is try to ignore their decline. Not only do many of us attempt this individually but culturally we also try with all our might to turn back the clock. Aging can become that "specter," wailing out in the open, reminding us we aren't immune to it. But sometimes, it is a whisper in the recesses of our subconscious where it has been long buried.

***

The Black Death certainly made the people of medieval Europe more aware of the reality that death comes to anyone, that death is the great leveler. But it also had an effect on the way people viewed the elderly and aging.

The large majority of medieval literature laments aging. Aging represents loss in many forms: weakness, depression, ill health, status, and loss of youthful "physical prowess."[5] Of course, most if not all medieval writers were men. In literary metaphors, the things that afflict man often take the form of a female: the crone, the witch, or the wicked old woman.[6]

Though our circumstances might be wildly different than the people in the Middle Ages, health and beauty have always been important to women and men have often misrepresented the reasons for it. In the Middle Ages, some men wrote mockingly about the use of cosmetics or beauty products to enhance the skin. To them, beauty care was, at best, the purview of women and at worst the purview of "disreputable old women" who were helping young women beautify themselves in order to ensnare a man.[7]

It shouldn't be surprising that age was a painful prospect during this time. People in the Middle Ages had fewer medical resources for pain management, disease, and decay. The medical community saw death as a natural process, but medieval theologians had a different perspective.[8] Saint Augustine viewed death as an unnatural state that came as the result of the fall, when Adam and Eve sinned and were led away from the garden (where they might've lived long or eternal lives). From this perspective, death and even aging were the result of and punishment for sin.[9]

While his view of aging can look harsh and depressing, if we place Augustine's views in contrast to our modern approaches to aging, the differences can be illuminating. Medieval society couldn't ignore "the perpetual presence of decay in all stages of life," and so they treated their elderly "as part of the community as a whole."[10] For example, elderly medieval Benedictine monks were given special tasks, their dietary needs were cared for, and they were not separated from the other monks. They were treated with compassion.[11]

In contrast, our current American culture is increasingly separated from its elderly and aging. When a friend from West Africa came to live with us, the first day he arrived he asked where Matthew's parents were. Matthew told him they were at their home in Missouri. Our friend had assumed Matthew's parents would be living with us because that was what generally happened in his culture. Certainly, there are very good reasons for some parents and their grown children *not* to live together, but it is revealing to note the difference. Not only do we view aging negatively but, as a whole, we are also more separate from the elderly than we once were.

A 2010 study of college students from twenty-six cultures offers further insights about the way our Western culture views the mystery of aging. What it found was that the participants who were from cultures with "greater Uncertainty Avoidance" (defined as a "low tolerance for ambiguity and endorsement of strict laws and rules as a means of stress reduction") tended to view aging more negatively.[12] The United States was in the bottom ten countries on its view of aging. In other words, our Western culture, with its distaste for ambiguity and its dependence on security and rules, had a more negative view of aging than the majority of countries listed.

This study reveals both that following rules makes us feel more secure and that we are uncomfortable with aging because it is uncontrollable. The things we cannot control or understand make us feel anxious, so we tuck into our rules and find comfort in the false hope that, maybe, we can stop our decay. But all the rule-following in the world cannot help us avoid the uncomfortable complexities of death. Our obsession with youth is wrapped up in the avoidance of uncertainty. It is just a way to numb ourselves against the mystery of our eventual decay.

In the 1970s, former US vice president Hubert Humphrey said that "The moral test of government is how that government treats those who are in the dawn of life, the children; those who are in the twilight of life, the elderly; those who are in the shadows of life, the sick, the needy and the handicapped."[13] There have been many iterations of this kind of quote: Fyodor Dostoevsky claimed a society should be judged on how we treat our criminals, and Gandhi said the same about how we treat our animals. These quotes all express a belief that the way we treat the most vulnerable among us reflects our moral values. The biblical mandate is clear in both the Old and New Testaments: God cares how God's people treat the widow, the orphan, and the stranger.

If how we view the elderly is a marker of the ways we are caring for all the members of our society, we might be in trouble. According to an international study in 2017, the elderly in the United States fare worse than eleven of the wealthiest other countries in the world, even with Medicare benefits.[14]

Do we fear age as a fiend, a wailing "specter" not unlike some of the terrors in our collective memory? Those horrific lines around our mouths and eyes, those grotesque gray hairs and loose bellies—we ward off these normal aspects of aging with our holy rose face water, fighting against them as if they were zombies, vampires, or skeletons trying to pull us down to the grave. We are terrified of aging. We spend millions of dollars to halt or hide our decay and become anxious when we cannot. Even after the beauty messaging has changed, even after new movements for body positivity, we still despise the changes in our bodies.

It's not that caring for our skin or bodies is bad, but our obsession with youth belies what we dread. That wailing specter isn't aging itself. We aren't just warding off aging in the here and now. The screaming monster that we are battling is the final decay of our bodies.

***

Even mystics are firmly lodged in the attitudes of their time and place. Though he was young by our standards, before he died at the age of forty-four, Saint Francis of Assisi was undoubtedly feeling the effects of aging and decay. He hadn't been well for some time. A life of poverty is not particularly good for a person's health. His body was bruised and sore from a climb up La Verna, an isolated mountain in Tuscany where he'd received the stigmata, the wounds of Jesus on his hands, feet, and side. His eyesight, weakened by disease, was nearly gone. Francis was suffering so much while he died that his confessor, Brother Leo, testified that, "in death Francis seemed like one just taken down from the cross."[15]

Aging and death weren't pleasant prospects for him. Saint Francis berated and often abused his body during his lifetime in a frustrated effort at spiritual discipline. The name he gave his body—"Brother Ass"—labeled it both as a sibling and as the Black Sheep of the family. But even Francis came to see his relationship with his body differently at the end of his life. The Community of Saint Francis tells the story this way. As his death drew near,

> Francis confessed to one of his brothers that he had an uneasy conscience about his care of his body, and was still afraid of indulging it too much in times of illness, anxious about providing for it delicacies or extra food. The brother responded by asking Francis how obedient had his body been through the years and the saint admitted that it was obedient in all things, "sparing itself nothing, rushing almost headlong to obedience; shirking no labor and refusing no discomfort." When the brother then asked Francis, "Where is your generosity toward your body?," Francis' reaction was to apologize to Brother Ass.[16]

Like many of his medieval counterparts, Saint Francis lamented aging, but he learned at the end of his life that his body had been a blessing. He knew that lamenting age and death is sometimes necessary in the face of pain and suffering. But thankfulness and grace are also antidotes to the terror of decay and age.

3

THE HORROR OF THE BODY

I've never been much fun at parties. Besides embodying the stereotype of an introvert who always knows the location of any corner at any party, I was *that kid* in middle school. The one who hated scary movies. The one who hid by the couch during a slumber party where twelve-year-old girls were allowed to watch the deeply disturbing television show *Tales from the Crypt*. This visual horror was followed up by a normally innocuous preteen game, "Light as a Feather, Stiff as a Board," which took on sinister and supernatural undertones after hearing victims get mowed down by demons and razor blades on TV for two hours.

Part of my problem was that I needed no help in imagining my own horrors. I did that just fine in the comfort of my bedroom: seeing demons in the wood grains of my closet, imagining that Freddy Krueger from the movie posters would get me in my nightmares.

It's no surprise, then, that when one of my family members died a few years ago, for a period of time, I couldn't stop imagining what his body would look like if it had been exhumed. A gruesome thought, to be sure. When I leafed through some pictures of "cadaver tombs" from the medieval period, I felt a peculiar sort of comfort that I wasn't the only one whose grief, at times, turned morbid. Surely those medieval sculptors, even as they made money from tombs commissioned by the rich, were also plumbing the depths of their own grief. When they crafted visual representations of the decomposing corpses of the dead, they drew on their own pain.

Cadaver tombs depicted what the body might've looked like weeks and months post-burial: flesh nearly gone, chest caved in, skeleton mouth hung open in a state of terror.[1] One particular cadaver tomb honored a prince who had died in war by creating a sculpture that imagined his rotting skeletal body with "shredded muscles falling from the bones and skin hanging in flaps over a hollow carcass." The carved corpse, for a time, actually held the prince's own dried heart (until it was stolen, oddly, and replaced with stone).[2]

As a whole, our Western world is unused to seeing death or being near dead bodies. I have yet to see a decomposing body depicted on a gravestone on my cemetery walks. I wonder if such a display would even be allowed in our more manicured places of the dead, which tend toward sculptures of angels or digital images of the deceased. As much as I love walking in them, our cemeteries are designed to give the most comfort possible to the grieving. Cadaver tombs had a different purpose.

Along with the *Danse Macabre*, cadaver tombs showed the medieval people that death was no respecter of persons. They also seem perfectly crafted for images in a modern horror film. Movies, books, and television shows that depict mass death scenarios or creatures in various stages of decomposition can find their locus in our collective memory of the horror of the Black Death and the art created in its wake. However, there is a difference between the way many such modern depictions are utilized and the way medieval folk viewed these gruesome images.

When modern viewers watch horror films, they have the luxury of remaining at a distance from the images. Maybe the pleasure in the grisliness is even enhanced with the relief they feel because they know that they are far removed from what is happening on screen. Maybe, if these viewers are really thoughtful, the films offer them a reminder that they will die. But still, horror films are so far from the realities of life that there is often a sense of "otherness" in watching horrifying images.[3]

On the other hand, death art for the people in the Middle Ages was intended to "stimulate anxiety."[4] The artists of cadaver tombs or other death art "would have failed in their purpose if their audiences had received the piece with the same sense of otherness."[5] Where modern Western viewers feel more removed from the realities of this horror, medieval audiences knew that at any moment, they could be "in the same putrefying condition, even perhaps, if one lived to be decrepit, while still alive."[6]

The horror captured in cadaver art seems to have acted as both therapy and a creative reflection on the shocks the viewers were experiencing. What does horror do for those of us who watch it now? Though I am still averse to watching horror movies, film critic Alissa Wilkinson says the genre challenges a fiction that modern audiences are telling themselves. "Horror burrows under our skin," Wilkinson writes, "because it clobbers one of the core principles we Modern People cling to: The world may be confusing, but it is ultimately knowable."[7] At its best, perhaps horror films approach what the medieval mind already knew: that life can be brutal and that death is inevitable and mysterious.

***

Medieval society had a decidedly strange relationship to the dead body, at least from our contemporary Western point of view. When it came to the bodies of saints, their relationship to the dead took on a heightened spiritual element because these saints' bodies concerned the connection between humans and God. They venerated the dead bodies of saints as if they still held something of import, as if there were something special and lasting and holy about even one tiny part of the body, like a tongue or, in some cases, a head.

Body reliquaries are containers that hold relics, items that represent something holy, a connection between humans and the sacred. Relics can be difficult to identify because they could be so many things: a bone, tongue, or tooth of a saint; a thorn from the crown laid on Christ's head; soil from a location considered spiritually significant. Art historian Cynthia Hahn goes so far as to say that a reliquary is "a space containing the ineffable."[8]

Body snatching, the mysterious locations of a saint's bones, and body displays (or their parts) have a wild and woolly history. Sixteenth-century Spanish saint Francis

Xavier's mummified corpse is on display under glass in India. Before it was put under this protection, pilgrims could actually kiss his corpse. One enthusiastic pilgrim might have even bit off his toe. In true saintly fashion, it was said to still be gushing blood.

Saint Anthony of Padua, a Portuguese saint who died of edema in Italy in the thirteenth century, was considered a stellar orator and had a gift for finding lost things. When his body was exhumed so it could be reburied in the basilica built for him, his corpse had decayed to dust. Except for his tongue. Which was apparently still moist.

Because of this intact tongue, Anthony was considered incorruptible, a term loosely assigned and loosely defined as a body that either doesn't decompose or experiences delayed decomposition. The incorruptibility of Anthony's mouth member was seen as a nod to his gift of speaking and preaching. Maybe it also blessed his knack for finding things. His tongue and jawbone—encased in a gold reliquary bust that looks like the chomping maw of a bejeweled zombie queen—were eventually put on glorious (or terrifying) display in the Basilica of Saint Anthony of Padua.[9]

The body of the beloved saint and mystic Francis of Assisi was venerated, stolen, and reburied. In the days after he died on October 3, 1226, Francis's body was placed in a tomb in the chapel of San Giorgio. Lying there in the chapel, his corpse attracted pilgrims who'd heard of his ministry and had seen the way he cared for lepers and other outcasts; they, too, were desperate for healing and redemption. His follower and hagiographer Thomas of Celano said "At his tomb . . . fresh miracles are constantly performing, and . . . the dead body heals living bodies, even as the living body raised up dead souls."[10] In other words, as scholar Jon Sweeney renders it: "His dead body heals those who are alive."[11] Francis's corpse became the locus for so many healings and miracles that just two years after his death, Pope Gregory declared him a saint.

Days before Francis's corpse was to be officially buried in a crypt in one part of the basilica, his friend Elias dug a new tomb for him elsewhere. He cracked and carved out the rock deep in the lower part of the church. There he laid Francis to rest and sealed up his coffin, dropping coins onto his grave. During the formal ceremony to inter Francis's body in the basilica, few knew that the coffin was actually empty.[12]

A little more than a century later, something similar happened to the body of Catherine of Siena, an Italian saint and mystic who lived in Tuscany. Catherine was born into the Benincasa family in the city of Siena, the staggering twenty-third child of her mother Lapa (who should be a saint for that alone). The date of her birth, March 25, seemed to be predictive of her mystical prodigiousness. In their pre-Gregorian calendar, March 25 was considered the conception date of Christ.

The fact that Catherine survived to adulthood was a miracle in itself. The Benincasa family somehow escaped the jaws of the Black Death when it swept through Europe the year after Catherine was born. It decimated the population of Siena (from forty-two thousand to fourteen thousand) by the time she was three.[13]

Catherine's mystical gifts announced themselves early. On a seemingly normal day when she was just six years old, Catherine had an unbelievably beautiful vision of a crowned Christ on his throne. Beside him were Peter,

Paul, and John the Evangelist. The vision was so comforting that when it was gone, poor Catherine, just a young little thing, began to berate herself for having made it go away.

This fierce and sometimes unforgiving piety would characterize the rest of Catherine's life. For many mystics, a single vision of Jesus transformed their life, leading to a single-minded (and sometimes unhealthy) obsession with encountering God again. This was true of Catherine. The trajectory of her young life now had but one focus: Jesus.

When the young Catherine cut off all of her hair to avoid a marriage, her parents finally allowed her to follow her spiritual vocation. Instead of entering a convent—like many young women who didn't marry—Catherine became a lay member of the Dominican Order of Penance. She secluded herself in a cell in her parents' home and experienced both terrible and glorious mystical visions. When, in once such vision, Jesus offered Catherine a ring, she entered what was termed a "spiritual marriage" with Jesus. Later, she received the stigmata like her predecessor Saint Francis, the wounds of Christ on her hands and feet.

When additional waves of the plague reached her town, Catherine nursed its victims, and the people attributed miracles of healing to her. Throughout her short adulthood, Catherine's religious power made her famous, and she wrote influential letters to both lay people and the pope, even daring to rebuke him when she didn't approve of his actions.

She spent the last two years of her life in Rome, beseeching those who controlled the church. She believed that the church would benefit from her work, though her insistent prayers had devastating effects on her body. When Catherine was just thirty-three, she had a massive stroke. At noon on April 29, Catherine of Siena made the sign of the cross and breathed her last.[14]

Catherine's confidants and followers knew that when her death was made public, the people would want to be near her body, to touch it, pray to it, venerate it. Despite their efforts to keep Catherine's death a secret, crowds gathered near her quickly. It was said that her body showed no significant signs of decay even though she wasn't buried for several days. Like Saint Francis, miracles and healings of pilgrims were attributed to the presence and power of Catherine's body, even after burial.[15]

Catherine was buried where she died, in Rome near the Pantheon in the cemetery of the Basilica di Santa Maria Sopra Minerva. Like Francis, Catherine's body was also reburied because of the concern of a friend. Her body was moved inside the basilica. It was during this reburial that her followers in Siena intervened, desperate to have their hometown holy woman laid to rest near them. They knew that if they stole her entire body, the theft would be noticed by the Roman guards. Instead, they broke her into pieces, severing her head and taking one of her thumbs.

The story goes that they hid her body parts in a bag as they attempted to smuggle them to Siena.[16] But the Roman guards were suspicious and blocked their way. In desperation, the body-part snatchers appealed to their beloved Catherine in prayer so that when the guards opened the bag, they saw not a severed head and thumb but a bag of sweet rose petals. When the thieves finally reached Siena, the miraculous petals had once again become a saintly head and thumb. Catherine's remains were put on display in her home church of San Domenico. You can still go there today and see her thumb resting near her mummified skull, adorned in a white wimple.

***

In the town of Kutná Hora in the Czech Republic, there is an ossuary chapel in the basement of a Gothic church. The word *ossuary* is from the Latin word for bone, and in the Sedlec Ossuary, bones are in great supply. In fact, they are used for decoration throughout the chapel, forming a chandelier, crosses, a family crest, and a chain across the entrance. The ossuary is decorated with the bones of some thirty thousand victims of the plague, bones that have been bleached and carved and continue to be cleaned individually with a toothbrush to keep them shiny.[17]

I wonder if our view of death would color the way we might see this staggering display of decorative bones or Catherine of Siena's head. Would we be horrified by the gruesomeness of Catherine's skull? Would we cringe at so many thousands of bones? Would we laugh the way my daughter laughed at the skull climbing the light fixture at the Halloween house? I gave a quick short laugh when I first saw a picture of Catherine's skull. And I felt a small measure of horror too.

For some pilgrims, like the ones who came to see the body of Saint Francis, relics represented a potential for physical healing. These body parts and even their containers offered a closer connection to God. Relics, thought to have a saint still dwelling in them, represented "intercession" between God and the pilgrim because "the saint is now in the court of heaven at the side of the resurrected Christ."[18] The saint's body parts made the spiritual connection between life and death, and between God and the seeking pilgrim, more tangible.[19]

To some contemporary museumgoers or pilgrims, reliquaries arouse a response that is similar to "elements of response to death itself."[20] These body parts of the saints and sculptured bones elicit a feeling inside us about death. Maybe our Halloween skeletons are the closest some of us will allow ourselves to get to body reliquaries: bones represent our bodies turned inside out, what's left of our bodies when our life has been peeled away.

You wouldn't be alone if you think that mummified and preserved bodies of saints are weird, gross, or maybe a little unholy. It's natural to find dead bodies and bones unpleasant and frightening. Though we might call the Sedlec Ossuary "creepy," bones didn't represent horror in the minds of the people of medieval times.[21] As they did in the ossuary, medieval people often presented these bones and human remains as decorative and even lovely.

Relics like Catherine's head or Saint Francis's body were important to medieval people because they actually "lead away from death and horror through intercession and access to salvation."[22] They brought comfort because they represented a life that was to come after all this death and destruction.

For all the visceral images of hell that came from the medieval period, the Christian view of the resurrection of the body gave Christians a concern for and interest in the body after death. In Christian theology, the body is of utmost importance. The resurrection of the body is central to Christian beliefs about life now and also life after death. If the Bible teaches that "Christ brought the reeking body of Lazarus out of the tomb into the midst of the living before his own resurrection (John 11:1–45)," then surely our rotting bodies were also important because of what would happen in eternity.[23] If our bodies were to be resurrected, then the body was more than just something to be shrugged off at death: "flesh and spirit would be reknit at the resurrection."[24]

The people who preserved the bodies of the saints were living in a culture that would probably feel chaotic and terrifying to us. Death and suffering couldn't be ignored. But they were not the only mysteries in the human experience. The people couldn't extract themselves from all the mysteries that haunted their lives. Illnesses could just as easily be attributed to spirits or demons as the weather could. Preserving the bodies of their holy people, something that would seem bizarre to us now, gave them a measure of connection with that mystery.

Whatever reaction these body reliquaries elicit from us, whatever ways we see cadaver tombs and the strange relationship the medieval people had with death, they offer a reminder—both of the limits of our mortal lives and of the ways people have understood and treated bodies, living and dead, throughout the centuries. They might also remind us that we are much more uncomfortable with the reality of death than our medieval counterparts.

When I imagined the decomposing body of my loved one, I was doing something that would've been more acceptable in the medieval world than in our culture. The people of the Middle Ages were much less averse to thinking about dead bodies. Theirs was a culture that plunged deeply into the grotesque and gruesome, not because it was necessarily obsessed with death but because it was forced to reckon with death. If we don't reckon with death until death hits us, we can be left unprepared, floundering in confusion.

4

ACTS OF LOVE

When I was a child, I developed a Band-Aid phobia. According to my mom, this fear reached its pinnacle when I stubbornly refused to keep the Band-Aids on that she'd applied to the oozing blisters on my feet, caused by those plastic jelly shoes from the 1980s. She didn't understand why I would rather keep the shoes on and let my blisters continue to break open and pustulate than wear a Band-Aid.[1]

Even now, the thought of used Band-Aids mashed into the dirt of the playground, the ones that flapped off of a child's ankle during play, or soiled bandages in the dusty corners of the public restroom makes me want to gag.

Maybe Band-Aids remind me of wounds. Wounds can be shocking to see and smell, visceral reminders that all those bloody, sinewy, bony parts peeking out underneath the skin are indeed mortal. I remember studying the Black Death in school; the descriptions of the wounds that accompanied such a horrible sickness dug their way into my psyche. Bursting boils or buboes the size of oranges on the groin or lymph nodes, symptoms that tortured the lungs or the blood, aches and pains across the eyes and the head.

The people of the Middle Ages were well acquainted with wounds. They didn't have the luxury of advanced medicine or science; doctors only had cursory knowledge, and their treatments often did more harm than good. Though they didn't always understand the science behind what caused bodies to die so violently with the Black Death or other illnesses, they saw what the skin of their failing children and parents and spouses looked like when boils bubbled and burst. They heard the sound of their cries and the agony of the silences when the cries stopped. Their acquaintance with disease and death was unavoidable; pain management a fiction.

For Saint Francis and Saint Catherine, an acquaintance with wounds and decay helped them approach the suffering of others. Saint Francis famously made peace with others' wounds. Growing up in a wealthy family, he was revolted (as many people were) by the lepers who were forced to remain on the edges of society. Wealth did for Francis what it has always done for those with power and resources: it allowed him to remain aloof from the suffering of others. As much as it was possible for a person in thirteenth-century Europe to avoid suffering, Francis did in his youth.

But his treatment of lepers became a marker of the blossoming of his relationship with God. And eventually, the leprosy that had formerly disgusted him became the evidence of his transformation.

One spring afternoon, Francis slid off his horse, reached out to a leper on the road, and kissed him. Only months later, he heard the voice of Jesus in the church at

San Damiano, and he moved toward a life of poverty, giving away all of his possessions and living with lepers.

Saint Catherine of Siena had a vision of Jesus in which she kissed and *licked* his wounds. This graphic image takes us from our tendency to spiritualize the passage in 1 Peter that says of Jesus, "by his wounds you have been healed." Catherine seemed, like many mystics, to believe not only in the spiritual but physical power of Christ's wounds.

There is also a story of a prisoner named Niccolo who was doomed for execution. By the time Catherine visited him in prison, he had already refused a priest and prayer. But Niccolo couldn't resist Catherine's charisma and contagious passion for God. When she finally got through to him, he begged her to become his confessor.

As Niccolo's beheading approached, he pleaded with her not to leave him. Catherine followed him up the long walk to the execution platform, heard his prayers, and knelt to catch his head as it was severed from his body.

As grotesque as these images might seem to us—of Catherine of Siena with her mouth to a wound and catching a decapitated head—she was offering her presence in death and decay.

Though I've never licked a wound—gross—I have tended to my children's wounds, hurts, and bodily fluids more times than I can count. I have cleaned up their vomit and feces, held bloody cuts closed with my hands. And while their wounds concerned me when they were severe, I can't imagine being *disgusted* by them. Band-Aids don't bother me when they have been on the cuts or wounds of my children.

Because I desperately love my children, even the unlovely parts of them are dear to me.

Even so, loving them can be challenging. But it is harder still to love others, especially those who might, at first glance, seem unlovable. Love has to be learned, tended, and nurtured if it is to be deep and lasting. Love expects us to care for the wounds of another, not just spiritually and emotionally but physically.

Saint Francis loved the wounds of others, but first he had to come to terms with his own wounds. Like all of us, he had to acknowledge that there were unlovely things about him too. He mourned his own weakness, and his love for others became so deep that he literally took on their wounds. Some say that the stigmata on his hands, feet, and side that oozed and never fully healed were actually leprous.

Becoming attuned to the things that disgust us and to the things that we fear is not just a good intellectual exercise. The ways we approach the things that horrify and disgust us might show the ways we look at death. The difficult and painful work of facing death can actually be an act of love.

5

A LIVING DEATH

After the cataclysmic horrors of the Black Death, life for the people of the Middle Ages would never be the same. Their lives would be forever upturned by those terrors. Their art, writing, religion, and ways of looking at the world would change shape. Many people turned to a mystical life of faith to find hope. Scholars believe that Julian of Norwich, an anchorite and mystic in fourteenth-century England, probably lost a husband and at least one child in one of the many Black Death epidemics.

In order to become an anchorite, Julian took vows entailing a demanding set of requirements that mostly added up to this: to be cut off from the rest of the world. After such a declaration, she lived out her life in a small cell or anchorage attached to a church, with only a narrow window connecting her to the outside world.

In the ceremony that declared her an anchorite—the "Rite of Enclosure"—a Requiem Mass, or funeral Mass, was performed. During her Mass for the dead, Julian was administered the last rites and then locked away in her anchorage, never to emerge again "under pain of excommunication."[1]

Having experienced the death of her family and community and taken vows to be declared dead in the eyes of the church, once in her anchorage Julian chose to embrace death further. She meditated on the details of Christ's death and desired to participate in his sufferings. In *Revelations of Divine Love*, she shares about enduring near-death illnesses that brought spectacular visions and revelations about God's goodness and love.

While Catherine of Siena found spiritual power in a medieval world where women had little power outside the convent or motherhood, Julian, too, offered a different vision of a woman's place in God's creation. Julian discovered in her visions that Jesus himself was not only our brother but also our mother. "God is our mother as truly as God is our father," she wrote. "Jesus is our true mother by nature, at our first creation, and he is our true mother in grace. . . . All the fair work and all the sweet, kind service of beloved motherhood is made proper to the second person."[2]

Though steeped in a medieval theology of the soul and afterlife like Dante's *Divine Comedy* and having lived through the gruesome and painful realities of the Black Death, Julian approached God, suffering, and her own death very differently than many around her. Not only did she look death in the face but she also saw a vision of God who was intimately involved with all aspects of the human experience. As Elizabeth MacDonald says in her book, *Skirting Heresy*: "In the smothering darkness, Julian hung out a lantern fired by the optimistic theology of the God of Love. She spoke of a God whose will shall be worked throughout creation, that the madness of earth is not the end of the story."[3]

Julian's message to a suffering world filled with horrors was to offer a brilliantly beautiful light. She told us that God was not only aware of the suffering of creation but was standing in it with an offering. Jesus came to Julian in the moments of her deepest pain and horror, even on her deathbed. He told her simply this: "All shall be well, and all shall be well, and all manner of things shall be well."[4]

***

The vast majority of anchorites in the late Middle Ages were women who voluntarily locked themselves away for life, never to leave on pain of excommunication. From a feminist perspective, one might understand the impetus to flee from the restraints put on women in the Middle Ages. Their sources of value came in their ability to bear children or pursue religious vocation. Being alone, and even, in a sense, choosing the hour of her death, was perhaps one of the few powers available to a woman.

But anchorites were also women of their time, bound and influenced by their culture, theologies, and church hierarchies. They were women of deep faith and conviction, and their decision wasn't made frivolously. Julian of Norwich had to gain permission to become an anchorite and submit herself to a thorough evaluation to ensure she was of sound mind and theology.

We might wonder if Julian was onto something, if her radical way of having a living death allowed her the space to have a vision of God that pushed the boundaries of orthodoxies. She showed herself to be both a woman of her time and one who occupied, in her mystical encounters with God, a place outside of time itself.

Julian didn't shy away from the horrors of the world and spoke clearly of hearing God's voice and letting God's words comfort and sustain her. She didn't shy away from speaking the truth, but humility still undergirded her words.

Women throughout history have often been told that humility is a feminine virtue. But perhaps more men of power and social standing ought to stare at their own graves for a few decades before they're allowed to speak a command. An awareness of death has the power to bring humility to anyone. And humility, more than any strict orthodoxy, could stay the hands of tyrants, kings, bishops, and presidents.[5]

PART II

SKULLS AND THE SUFFERING GOD: EARLY MODERN MYSTICS AND THE FEAR OF DEATH

6

THE SCORCHES OF PREDESTINATION

When I entered the theater with my family, the lights were so low that it took a moment for our eyes to adjust to the images filling the room. On one side of the room, the pictures were in soft colors: whites and yellows, greens and blues. As our eyes scanned around the space, reds and oranges whipped up, flapping in the shape of a ribbon in the wind.

The images that emerged in the last set of colors were abrupt and disturbing: the deep scorches of blood and fire. Torture and the executioner's tools tore at skin, blood leaked out of severed heads, and fire blistered at the feet of bodies being burned to death.

You might think we were watching a horror film.

Instead, Matthew, our kids, and I were touring a quaint Anabaptist heritage center in Amish country. The colorful and violent images were from a painting called *Behalt*, a cyclorama displayed all the way around a large, dimly lit room. An Amish man, dressed in traditional, plain clothes and sporting a chin curtain, was our docent. He explained the origins of the painting and pointed out some of the scenes it depicted.

Behalt was painted by a man named Heinz Gaugel beginning in the 1970s. Gaugel was Catholic, but he was attracted to the Amish and their Anabaptist views of nonviolence. He painted a visual story of the Christian church—from creation to the second coming of Christ—from an Anabaptist perspective. Some of Gaugel's painting depicts the hopes of the Christian church. But about the time of the Reformation, when the red and orange colors take over, things get gruesome, not only in the painting but in the darker parts of the church's past.[1]

The Reformation of the sixteenth century was not the church's finest hour. Certainly, men like Martin Luther brought important and necessary reforms to an increasingly corrupted church. But there was the violence. Christians were killing each other. Christians were killing non-Christians. They indulged their basest instincts: gutting, hanging, torture, war, and even occasionally defenestration, a punishment bizarrely modeled after the execution of Jezebel in the Old Testament in which people push each other out the window. It's hard to understand how such violence could be done in the name of Jesus, the Prince of Peace, but it wouldn't be the first or the last time that humans killed in God's name.

The main characters that thread through *Behalt* are a group of Christians called Anabaptists. Considered the left wing of the Reformation, they were condemned by both Catholics and Protestants.

One of those early Anabaptists was a German Benedictine monk named Michael Sattler who left the monastery during the German Peasants' War. He married Margaretha, who had been a member of a group of women called the Beguines.

The Beguines were a religious sisterhood not officially attached by vows to the church. They lived in communities throughout Europe from the thirteenth through sixteenth centuries and formed their own fully functioning settlements. Unified by their deep longing and love for God, the Beguines produced some beautiful works of mystical poetry and writing.[2] A few of them were actually killed because of their writings.

Only months after Sattler and his peers produced their statement of Anabaptist beliefs, he, his wife Margaretha, and others were imprisoned and executed. In Michael Sattler's last moments, he prayed for his torturers. Just before his tongue was cut out, he was scorched with hot tongs. Then he was burned at the stake.

Thankfully, this violence was of little interest to my two youngest children who were bored by the painting *Behalt* and wandered over to a few antique farming implements they weren't supposed to touch. But my eight-year-old son Jude, who is interested in death anyway, was mesmerized. The docent briefly mentioned the torture and killing depicted in the painting, but I could tell my son wanted to know more. "Mom," he whispered, "are they cutting that guy's head off?"

I recalled how many times in the history of the Western world innocent people have become scapegoats for our fears. During the Black Death, entire Jewish communities were slaughtered by mobs or collectively burned at the stake.[3] Muslims in the United States were the victims of hate crimes after the attacks on September 11, 2001. Immigrants have repeatedly been mischaracterized as criminals in the United States and all over the world.

I felt a measure of fear and queasiness when I looked at those images, reminiscent of the time when I was pressured into watching *Tales from the Crypt* during that sleepover. Or when my father decided it was a good idea to drag the family, when I was a preteen, on a Jack the Ripper tour through London.

My instinct is to shield my children from all of the world's horrors. Isn't that the wish of most parents? As sheltered as the Amish and conservative Mennonites might seem to those of us who aren't a part of their culture, there is a tradition in Anabaptism of allowing kids to witness some of the horrors in our history.

Martyrs Mirror—a book written in the seventeenth century that tells the stories of those killed for their faith (especially Anabaptists)—has been bedtime reading material for Anabaptist children for generations. Their parents wanted them to understand the cost their ancestors paid for their faith.

One of the most famous stories in *Martyrs Mirror* is about Dirk Willems, an Anabaptist in sixteenth-century Holland who was imprisoned, tried, and convicted for his belief that adults, and not infants, should be baptized. Willems escaped from prison by dropping out of a window and landing on the ice-covered moat that surrounded the fortress. Because Willems was malnourished, his weight didn't break through the ice, and he crossed it safely. But a palace guard, who ran after him, wasn't so lucky. Instead of continuing to run and assuring his escape, Willems turned back and rescued the guard. Despite saving the guard's life, Willems was taken back to prison and burned at the stake.[4]

This story is popular among Anabaptists because it offers a real-life example of someone who loved his enemy, who put the life of another above his own life. Like the saints of the Catholic church, the men and women of *Martyrs Mirror* are the Anabaptist saints, offering examples of people who really lived out their faith, even when it meant they could die.

Martyrs Mirror and the twentieth-century painting *Behalt* are, in a way, both throwbacks to the medieval memento mori. And not coincidentally, *behalt* actually means "to remember." The painting and book spare no gruesome detail of Sattler's death. But instead of simply reminding us that we are going to die, these memento mori go a step further: they remind Christians why their ancestors *chose* to die.

***

After the sixteenth century, the church would never be catholic again. It would continue to be Catholic—the Counter-Reformation would see to that—but now the lowercase term *catholic*, which derived from Greek and/or Latin to mean "universal," could no longer apply to the split, tattered, tortured body of Christ. And the view of that tortured body (both the church and Jesus Christ) would also change the way people saw their own bodies and their mortality.

Humanism, a philosophy that adopted the ideas and attitudes from Greek and Roman antiquity, had a great influence on the Protestant Reformation. In contrast to what many reformers had seen as the dogma and unclenching authority of the Catholic Church, Christian humanists (many of them reformers) rejected hierarchy in favor of the individual, who could stand before God without a mediator.[5]

Christian humanists saw the mind as reasonable, able to grasp the significance of the idea of life and death and "once having done so, [able to] reason that life and death are the same, and that dying well is therefore only an extension of living well."[6] In this way of thinking, the fear of death seemed irrational. Or worse, a damnable offense.

In the culture of the medieval period, when death could come so swiftly, the church formed a series of rituals that offered souls a second chance at redemption. A deathbed confession, a last-minute cleansing of the soul, was common. But by the Reformation of the sixteenth century, both Catholics and Protestants discouraged this last-minute soul preparation in favor of a lifelong religious piety. Fear of death, in this context, indicated that someone hadn't lived a holy life, otherwise, why would they be afraid of the afterlife?[7]

Reformed theologians, and particularly Calvinists who believed in the theology of predestination, viewed fear as "a sign of doubt, and doubt a sign of damnation."[8] A heroic (and godly) death was therefore faced without trepidation of either death or the afterlife because the dying person was right with God. Therefore, while the people of the Middle Ages tended to accept that fear was understandable because death could be swift or gruesome, in the more rational view of the Reformation, fear of death became something to hide and be ashamed of.

This changing approach to the fear of death during the Reformation is reflected in graveyard art and the artistic depictions of death. The decaying corpse portrayed in medieval cadaver tombs was exchanged for a skeleton: bony and skinless. And instead of dancing with its victims out in the open like the *Danse Macabre*, this skeletal depiction of Death began to conceal itself from its prey.

Artists of the Reformation were making tangible what was happening in the human psyche. The medieval vision of a dancing Death, the unconquerable great leveler, was replaced by a crouching, prowling Death that left its victims with a "sense of pervasive death—the intangible threat lurking in every corner."[9] As the fear of death became taboo, the figure of Death hid away, waiting and watching.

Eventually, though, the skeleton lost its entire body, and the lone skull became representative of death instead. Curiously, it became so fashionable to wear the skull as jewelry that prostitutes began wearing them, at first to fit in with fashion. The skull was so ubiquitous among prostitutes that it became a symbol of their profession.[10] Did prostitutes also use the skull for reasons beyond fashion? Did they understand that the commodifying of sex could be a form of death fear?

The skull is bodiless. It cannot lurk or prowl anymore. It becomes just a flaccid, unthreatening symbol, even a fashion statement. The symbol had seemingly lost its outward terror and, at times, represented something else.[11] The skull, according to author Phoebe S. Spinrad, was "not a reminder of death but a protection against it, a lucky charm that would allow the wearer to forget about death."[12]

But death cannot be avoided just by forgetting. The more we try to repress thoughts of death, the more our fears lodge themselves into our subconscious, waiting to emerge when they're ready.

***

I struggled with obsessive thoughts and anxious fears as a child. When I was very young, I started refusing to go anywhere alone, even to the bathroom in our house. My anxiety got so bad that my mom took me to a psychologist when I was four. I still remember that my psychologist used *Sesame Street* puppets to draw me out. And my mom remembers the way I skipped out of the office afterward, all by myself.

Childhood fears are, of course, a normal part of brain development and an increasing awareness of aspects of death. At the age of four, most children start to understand the first aspect: the irreversibility of death, that once dead, a person cannot return. Between the ages of five and seven, children begin to understand both the nonfunctionality of death (that a dead person cannot eat, drink, or be sad) and the universality of death (that everyone dies).[13]

Many children don't start to actually fear death until they reach later elementary school when their understandings of death are a bit more realistic. As we grow, we can repress death and the fear of death, especially if our culture is designed to ignore death.

When I was experiencing anxious thoughts, I believed that even having a negative thought was bad and meant I was more likely to act on it. The fear and guilt made the thoughts worse, and they became intrusive and cyclical. Psychoanalysis suggests that people with intrusive thoughts will often try to suppress them. But suppression can actually lead to a greater frequency of the intrusive thoughts and a greater anxiety associated with them.[14]

If the fear of death during the Reformation became attached to damnation then it stands to reason that this might have led to the suppression of fear. Suppression would have become a defense mechanism against thoughts and fears that, if expressed, had dangerous consequences. Because the suppression of a natural fear can turn the fear into something bigger and more monstrous, suppression often leads to anxiety or neurosis. One way to cope is to find other ways to express your fears—and many people during the Reformation did just that. During the sixteenth century and beyond, other symbols outside the church began to emerge to "transfer the fear into a related expression, one that [could] be worked through."[15]

Death anxiety was reassigned "to the passage of time, to Time the Destroyer. Rather than lamenting one's own end, one could now lament the end of all beautiful things—and the more beautiful and fragile, the better."[16] This change wasn't necessarily unhealthy. People still mourned, even if what they were mourning was the collective end of all things instead of our individual demise. But time, like the skull or the skeleton, is really only a placeholder for death. These placeholders reflect the culture and the theological approaches to death, but, in the end, they are just more creative coping mechanisms for death. As Spinrad says: "One cannot face the faceless."[17]

***

On the wooden bench of a Jesuit college in Paris, a young man named Francis leaned forward in his seat to take in the details of a discussion. A debate had erupted in the room, men arguing over a doctrine (as they do) that had been recently stirred up by the Reformation. Had God ordained eternity for every person? Had God predestined heaven or hell for each of us?

Francis had never considered that his eternal home might be in question. After all, as the firstborn of thirteen children, educated in law and theology in the finest of schools, he was morally fastidious. He followed all Catholic teachings. He memorized Scripture, he prayed, and he supported all of the church's teachings. Surely he would be a shoo-in for heaven. Even so, something about the discussion began to nag at him.

Without warning, the word *predestination* appeared in his mind's eye.

What if his arrogance and pride outweighed his righteous deeds? What if none of his works mattered because he was condemned anyway?

He batted at the word with his hand, as if swatting a fly, and refocused on the debate, which was intensifying. But the word popped up again, this time forming the phrase *predestined for hell* across his brain, letter by letter, as if the invisible hand from Daniel had written it on the wall of his mind. He could almost see it hanging there in the air in front of him, dangling over the head of the lecturer.

"Stop!" he whispered fervently, attracting the looks of his nearest peers. But the words flicked back so that no matter where he turned, he could see them.

He felt a gentle warmth crawling up the base of his spine, like the early sparks of a hearth fire. But the warmth was not gentle for long.

I am predestined for hell. The words began to taunt him.

Francis tried to drag the words away by reciting a psalm, scrubbing away these hot, red, bleeding letters with the ancient poetry of David. But they came back insistently, a twitch at first, then a stutter, then they began to spin in a circle, round and round, so fast that the sparks from his spine flared together with the flaming words in recognition, in mutuality of purpose. The heat built and rose, the words flaming in his body. He felt them in his neck and shoulders, hot and tingly with certainty: they were going to burn him up in eternal torment. For if he was indeed predestined for hell then surely that hell, which *was* and *is* and *is to come*, began now, in this moment. He was predestined to burn, *always*.

Francis stood abruptly from the bench so that the wood and stone scraped against one another with a loud and heavy shriek. The noise echoed throughout the lecture hall.

The debate ceased abruptly. He pushed past his fellow students with only a peripheral awareness of the interruption he'd caused, an interruption that would normally have mortified him. He rushed out of the arched doorway and followed the meandering stone corridors of the college, unaware of his surroundings, until he finally reached the place that always soothed his mind. The inner courtyard of the college was square and clipped, meticulously hedged and molded into the neat outline of the building's corners. He leaned a forearm against the wall, breathing in huffs and pants, urging the coolness of the stone into the fire that was burning him up inside. The flames quieted until the tidy coolness of the stone finally doused out the fire.[18]

He walked slowly back to his rooms, relishing the relief he felt.

But as he undressed for bed, hanging up his school robes, he felt an exhaustion he didn't understand. He lay down in bed and snuffed out the light of the candle. But behind his closed eyes, he saw the flames of hellfire dancing like a sneer. They climbed out of his dreams and into his body until he was sure again that he would burn for eternity.

For days, weeks, months, he awoke to flames, he ate to flames, he sang and he prayed to them, bathed in them, and barely slept. He became so hot that he was bedridden for days at a time.

Every prayer he prayed begging for release only sent him deeper into the heat, the fear, the certainty that he was doomed for the eternal torment of hell.

Then one evening during vespers, ill and exhausted, longing for comfort, he knelt at the foot of a statue of Mary, *Our Lady of Good Deliverance*. Mary, a crown on her head, adorned in multicolored robes of red, blue, and gold, looked down at him. Her eyes bore into Francis's soul. They knew him. They saw and loved him, just as a mother would. Francis suddenly knew that Mary was *his* mother. She nurtured him, loved him, carried him, and held him.

Francis sank to his knees, and between sobs, he prayed: "Remember, O most gracious Virgin Mary, that never was it known that anyone who fled to thy protection, implored thy help, or sought thine intercession was left unaided." Then he begged, "O Mother of the Word Incarnate, despise not my petitions, but in thy mercy hear and answer me."[19]

When he finished the prayer, he sank further down. A scorching fire, even more painful than before, burned through him, starting at his toes. Inch-by-inch it climbed up his body until it reached the top of his head. When he thought he couldn't bear the agony a moment longer, the fire erupted out of the top of his head and then blew away in the breeze from the open window. The heat had been extinguished. Finally. Before Mary he knew he was indeed delivered; before Jesus, he was reborn. The comfort and peace overwhelmed him with joy.

Saint Francis de Sales was nineteen when he had a mystical experience at the feet of Mary, the "Black Madonna of Paris," at the parish of Saint-Étienne-des-Grès. The calm and assurance he felt at that moment, freeing him from weeks and months of torment, stayed with him the rest of his life.

A few years after this mystical experience, he became a priest and fervently worked to spread Catholicism in the Counter-Reformation, a time when the Catholic Church reaffirmed many of the values and beliefs that had been threatened by the reformers—doctrines and ideals like purgatory, the priesthood, and the importance of church tradition. Francis de Sales preached against Calvinism, perhaps as a reaction against the Calvinist emphasis on predestination that had so tormented him.

After he became the bishop of Geneva at the age of thirty-five, his pastoral ministry began in earnest. His reputation grew as a gentle and compassionate counselor. One of the most moving pieces of de Sales's writing is his picture of God as a nursing mother, one who offers infinite nurture and care to her children. I can imagine that as he was writing that beautiful passage about the feminine nature of God, he recalled the healing he experienced at the foot of Mary.

While many of his theological peers emphasized the depravity of humanity, Saint Francis de Sales had been moved by his internal torment to see humans as inherently good. His theological culture was steeped in the belief that the fear of death was cowardly or even that it indicated damnation. In contrast, de Sales had scores of writings—many of them letters to those who sought his council—offering comfort and gentle words about death.

Francis de Sales was certainly rigorous in his faith and held firmly to the traditional beliefs of the Catholic Church—of heaven and hell and the need to be saved by God. At the same time, he drew comfort from meditating on the goodness and love of God. In a section of his writings entitled "Remedies Against Excessive Fear of Death," de Sales urges readers to avoid books discussing "death, judgment, and Hell" as an incentive for faith. As an antidote to excessive fear, he taught people to be "fully resolved to live in a Christian manner, and have no need of being impelled to it by motives of fear and terror."[20] He didn't shy away from the truth that death could be "hideous." But, for de Sales, the life "beyond the grave" was something to anticipate because we get to be with a loving and merciful God after death.[21]

Francis de Sales's love and generosity placed him among the most popular and beloved of saints, both in his time and even today. One of his biographers said that his piety and devotion never overtook his kindness. His "sweetness [appeared] without weakness, and his firmness without bitterness."[22] Saint Francis de Sales was marked by his own suffering, and it offered him an unparalleled compassion for the suffering of others.

***

When I was a child terrified in the darkness, tugging at my mother's arm, hoping to get her to stay in my room with me all night, or later when I was a young mother suffering with anxiety and depression, she would recite psalms to me. One of our favorites was Psalm 34: "I sought the Lord, and he answered me; / he delivered me from all my fears" (v. 4). I have found a lot of solace in the biblical psalms, in well-known verses like the one from Psalm 23: "Even though I walk through the valley of the shadow of death, / I will fear no evil" (v. 4 ESV) or "Be still, and know that I am God," from Psalm 46 (v. 10).

Saint Francis de Sales was steeped in these psalms, so much that he quoted them when his death drew near. After de Sales suffered a seizure, one of his visitors expressed sadness at his dying. De Sales replied with the words of Psalm 40:1,[23] "I waited patiently for the Lord; / he turned to me and heard my cry."

The next verses of the psalm are poignant, given what we know about Francis de Sales's early life and fears:

> He lifted me out of the slimy pit,
> out of the mud and mire;
> he set my feet on a rock
> and gave me a firm place to stand.
> He put a new song in my mouth,
> a hymn of praise to our God. (vv. 2–3)

One of the messages theologians gave to the people of the early modern period was that they should not be afraid of death, or else they risked fear of damnation. Steeped in these theologies and fears, I imagine Saint Frances de Sales wasn't alone in the anxiety and terror he felt in his youth. Isn't it human to be afraid of the things we don't understand? For those of us who might struggle with fear of death, de Sales's last few words could be a comfort. He was no longer afraid. He looked forward to his reunion with the God of Psalm 89—another passage he quoted near death.[24] "I will sing of the Lord's great love forever; / with my mouth I will make your faithfulness known / through all generations" (v. 1). Francis felt rescued. He saw that the God of love, who had lived, died, and was resurrected, had freed him from the mud and mire of fear and given him refuge and rest.

7

WOUNDS OF RESURRECTION

When I saw my grandmother Oneta's body for the first time after she died, laid out in her hospice bed, her hands had already lost their color and warmth. But they had not lost their distinctive shape. Through all of my childhood memories of her, arthritis had bent my maternal grandmother's fingers and joints in sideways angles and painful knots, bulging like knobs on an otherworldly tree trunk. Like those trees, her hands always held some rooted magic for me.

Covered in brightly colored costume rings and a silver band that she mischievously called her "poison ring" because it had a hidden compartment, her hands clicked and chimed when she moved. Her fingers rested against her cheek or tapped her long, pointed nose, gracefully curled even though they were crooked. She began to paint when she was in her sixties. Her hands were always casting spells of creation, lifting and brightening our world and her own like a lovely old witchwoman might through magic.[1]

In the weeks before she went into hospice care, she had a series of strokes that left her writhing in pain and largely unresponsive. The doctor asked my mom, uncle, and grandfather what Oneta's wishes were for resuscitation. My grandmother was in her nineties, and she'd recently had two emergency vascular surgeries. When she woke up from surgery and realized she was still alive, she'd gotten angry and yelled at the nurses that they hadn't let her just go ahead and die. It was therefore agreed: she did not want any medical intervention.

I was single and in my late twenties at the time of her death. I'd recently returned to my home state of Texas to process the emotional and spiritual shifts that came from four years in graduate school in Scotland. Generations of my family grew out of the soil of tenant farms, small towns, and isolated acreages in dusty West Texas where my ancestors worked the drought-weary land past its usefulness. Their lonely children grew up melancholy and longing to leave. That's how my family had eventually migrated farther south, and I'd grown up in the cedar-lined hills of Austin.

Oneta, raised in a small Texas town and unmarried until she was thirty, was a kindred spirit. For a year before grad school, I lived down the street from her. I dropped in on her from time to time and usually found her in the cool side room off the garage, putting the finishing strokes on a painting she was making for my sister. She was always glad to see me, and she always left her work when I came over.

After she kissed me, she'd usually go straight to the

fridge and make us both our favorite cold beverage: Diet Dr Pepper mixed with white wine. It sounds disgusting now, but we both loved how rebellious it made us feel at the time. My conservative grandfather would shake his head in mild disapproval while we metaphorically thumbed our noses at him and drank a glass of wine at eleven o'clock in the morning.

When I arrived at the hospital after Oneta's stroke, my mom and I spent the night in her room. Mom, vigilant in carrying out my grandmother's wishes, corrected a technician who mistakenly tried to test her for pneumonia. The next day they moved her by ambulance to a hospice facility.

When she was settled into her hospice room, the nurses hooked her up to a morphine drip and encouraged us to get some rest. And my grandmother did what she'd often done in life: stubbornly refused to let go, even though she'd said she wanted to. I also think she lingered because she hated to say goodbye to us, her beloveds.

Or maybe she was afraid. She'd expressed at vulnerable and sober moments that she hoped God would forgive her for her sins. She was raised in the hellfire-and-brimstone preaching era of her church tradition, and the fear of not being right with God still lingered from childhood as it had for Saint Francis de Sales.

She had a deep zest for life, but as she got older, she would tell my mom that she knew it was her job to prepare us for her own eventual death.

Oneta would say: "It's time to pass on the torch."

My mom would reply: "You keep trying to pass the torch to me, and I keep trying to pass it back."

Oneta would tell my mother not to feel guilty that she

didn't need her anymore. That's the cycle of life and generations, she would say—we work ourselves out of a job so that our loved ones can let us go.

Toward the end of her life, my grandmother told us that her beloved mother appeared to her at night. They had very pleasant conversations. Sometimes Oneta talked about dying as the next adventure. "I don't know what it's going to be like," she'd say to us. "I'm looking forward to it." Still, she would mourn that she wouldn't be able to see what happened to all of us, to see us marry or have children or make our small marks in the world.

Over the next few days in hospice, Oneta crossed into active dying. Because she wasn't eating or drinking, she became skeletal and pale. Then she developed a "death rattle"—the sounds made when a patient is unable to swallow anymore and secretions collect in the upper chest and throat.

On her last night, Mom sat by my grandmother's side. The hospice nurse told my mom that, despite Oneta's near-death state, it was likely my grandmother could hear her. So my mom talked to my grandmother, acting as her death midwife, whispering words of affirmation about what a good mother and grandmother she'd always been. She told her she "would always remember her love, her sayings, and her wisdom." In the same way Oneta had helped my mom through the labors of her children, my mother eased her mother down the labored path of death.

I've heard hospice workers say that patients often wait until their family members leave the room to die. That is what happened to my grandmother. About an hour after my mom went home to rest, Oneta died of another massive stroke.

When I saw her for the first time after she died, the hospice nurse who'd found her dead in the small hours of that January morning had arranged her body more neatly. Our professional midwives of death must do their work to make our loved ones' bodies presentable to us. Eyes of the dead do not always close on their own, bodies do not always lie back gracefully.

People sometimes say of their deceased loved ones, "She looked so peaceful she could've been sleeping," but my grandmother did not look asleep. At her death, my grandmother looked like her spirit had broken free and left a husk of bones and skin behind. It was hard to imagine, in that moment, that one day her body would come alive again, resurrected in glory.

***

Nearly a decade after Oneta's death, on the last night of vacation with my extended family in Colorado, only hours before Matthew and I would be flying back to Illinois, my father told us that he had been diagnosed with cancer.

We returned home to Illinois in a haze, trying to make sense of the diagnosis, trying to process our fears. The next spring, while my father was undergoing all kinds of cancer treatments, Matthew was thinking through his sermons for Lent and Easter. Lent's focus on suffering, deprivation, and the coming wounds of Jesus wasn't far from the realities since my father's cancer diagnosis: surgery, chemotherapy, radiation, the failure of his natural killer cells.

Our dinnertime conversations turned to Jesus's

appearance to the disciples after his resurrection, to the episode where poor Thomas was saddled with his unfortunate moniker: "Doubter."[2] The Italian artist Caravaggio—considered by some to be one of the greatest painters of all time—painted a terribly potent picture of Thomas probing Jesus's resurrection wounds. In the painting, *The Incredulity of Saint Thomas*, he reaches to touch his Lord's flesh. The skin of Jesus curves over Thomas's fingers as he leans in to inspect the wound on Jesus's side. This painting was one of many biblical stories depicted by Caravaggio in a starkly lit, realistic, and fleshly style.

At the height of Caravaggio's career, the Counter-Reformation of the late sixteenth and early seventeenth centuries was furiously fortifying itself against Protestants' attacks on its doctrine. The Catholic Church wanted art that showed biblical stories in ways that were doctrinally sound, that could act as a visual affirmation of Catholic doctrine for the masses. Caravaggio's commitment to the theologies of the Council of Trent in his paintings put him in good standing with many of the Catholic authorities. But the naturalism of his paintings, his realistic rendering of the sacred, was also controversial.

There was a stark violence and bleakness to many of Caravaggio's paintings. This bleakness wasn't surprising to me when I began to read about his life. His biography was erratic, violent, and brief. Though his family was financially well off, he was no stranger to famine or disease. His father and grandfather died in another brutal cycle of the plague when he was just six years old. In his adult years, Caravaggio's prison rap sheet was long:

drunkenness, affairs with prostitutes, brawls, possession of illegal weapons, and confrontations with police. He was an early modern Goth, dressing in black and walking the streets of Rome with his black dog, Crow, "brandishing swords and daggers at the slightest provocation."[3] He murdered a man during a fight gone wrong.

His short life was a frenzied contrast of violence and creativity, of painting techniques so original that he changed the art form. Not long after another fight that left him profoundly disfigured, he died at the age of thirty-eight. His body was found only a decade ago when a cemetery in Tuscany was excavated for his remains. His cause of death is still debated.

Caravaggio was accustomed to the violence of Rome, where he made his home for a while. A theme that found its way into many of his paintings might have been influenced by Rome's almost daily public executions. Caravaggio displayed a disturbing fixation on the severed head. This is perhaps most viscerally evident in *Judith Beheading Holofernes*, a painting based on the apocryphal book of Judith. Included in the Catholic and Orthodox Old Testament canon, the book tells of a woman who saves her people from a Syrian general by killing him in his sleep. The painting spares no gory detail, as blood spurts from the neck of the general, his face contorted in agony as he dies.

Another biblical beheading, Caravaggio's *David with the Head of Goliath*, was actually painted as a petition for pardon when Caravaggio fatally stabbed a man after a drunken brawl. Caravaggio made the dripping severed head of Goliath into a self-portrait. The pardon was granted. We might wonder what Caravaggio was saying by portraying himself as a classic biblical bully who came to a gruesome end. Some of it is probably obvious: by putting himself as the dead villain, he was making a confessional plea for his life. But was he also making a statement about his sin? Was he sorry?

A few years before the murder, Caravaggio was commissioned to paint an entirely different scene of biblical characters. *The Death of the Virgin* is both a departure from the gruesomeness of his other works and further evidence of his understanding of death. Caravaggio was commissioned to paint it for a Catholic order of Discalced Carmelites. The painting depicts the corpse of Mary, the Mother of Jesus, surrounded by apostles on her deathbed.[4]

Caravaggio's depiction of Mary might be strange to anyone used to seeing pious and glorious representations of her. In the painting, Mary's skin is pale, and her body shows the physical indications of death, bloating and discoloration. One scholar says that Caravaggio's painting of Mary's corpse "is a true portrayal of death . . . painted with stark naturalism. Hers is an exhausted, swollen body whose naked feet and ankles project stiffly from beneath the coverlet, yet one that lacks neither grace nor dignity."[5]

And yet, the Carmelites who commissioned *The Death of the Virgin* declined the painting after it was finished. Caravaggio was devastated. Some claimed that the refusal of the painting was because Mary's bloated appearance was too realistic, too profane for the nuns. Others think it was because of Caravaggio's choice of model. For Mary, the Mother of God, Caravaggio used the corpse of a prostitute who had drowned.

To modern scholars, this painting of Mary tells something of Caravaggio's understanding of the great and terrible mystery, that death is depicted as "illumination."[6] Caravaggio undoubtedly knew something about death, particularly death at its most vile, violent, and wounded. I don't imagine I would've wanted anything to do with him in real life, but something about Caravaggio's art still moves me. He was a brilliant but wounded soul, intent on his own destruction.

Though his depiction of doubting Thomas is probably not a self-portrait like the headless Goliath, I wonder if Caravaggio saw something of himself in Thomas too. That particular painting of Thomas shoving his finger into Jesus's side is a bit like what Caravaggio did in his art: he stabbed into the biblical stories, curiously digging around, looking for illumination and understanding. Looking, perhaps, for himself.

When Matthew and I talked about Caravaggio's Thomas painting during Lent, there was something particularly poignant about the subject matter: about wounds and scars, about death, and about resurrection. Especially in light of my father's cancer diagnosis.

Many Christians, if we think about resurrection much at all, tend to imagine our future resurrected bodies a bit Platonically: the best images of ourselves, at our most beautiful and healthy. But I wonder if that's how it will be.

As I thought about scars and wounds and my father's diagnosis, it struck me that Jesus's resurrected body betrays the myth of our vague views of resurrection. Caravaggio was depicting a clearer version of a resurrected body: Jesus's new body wasn't whole and pristine but riddled with scars, maybe even open wounds.

If Jesus didn't shrug off his wounds, maybe we shouldn't see our scars and wounds as things that need to be erased in the resurrection. One of my favorite spiritual writers, Henri Nouwen, says that "What we have lived in our body will not go to waste but will be lifted up in our eternal life with God."[7] Theologian N. T. Wright goes further, saying: "The risen Jesus was more human, not less, than he was before."[8] For the abused and mistreated, the sick and dying, the anxious and depressed, our emotional and physical wounds, whatever form they take in resurrection, could be striking reminders that we are not less because of our hurts.

Maybe this kind of resurrection is still not good news to everyone. Maybe it's a horrifying thought, but I wonder if all of our wounds will be on full display and we will examine one another like Thomas did, not in sick fascination but as a way to see God's glory in the prominence of our true humanity. My grandmother's arthritis might be healed in eternity, or maybe there will be the shadow of calluses from her painter's brush on her fingers.

As for Caravaggio, I am touched by Jesus's response to Thomas in his painting. The painted Christ grabs hold of the doubter's hand and pulls it closer, inviting him to look, feel, and understand. Maybe Caravaggio's understanding of the violence done to the body gave him a deeper understanding of what bodily resurrection would be like. Maybe it gave him hope, even for himself and all of his self-destructive behaviors. Jesus's resurrection invites us away from the hatred or mistrust of the body. His resurrection calls us to a deeper love and care of our bodies, to see our bodies not as things to be cast off at death but as part of our eternal life. That resurrection is the embodied invitation of Jesus for all humans to enter into his own body, even with our dirtiness, our violence, our soiled hands, and our profound disbelief.

8

LESSER DEATHS

In the mid-seventeenth century, Caravaggio wasn't the only Italian artist depicting religious figures in both orthodox and subversive ways. The artist Bernini was born in Naples, Italy, just over a decade before Caravaggio's untimely death. After Caravaggio fled Rome for Naples because he'd murdered a man, it's possible that he was in Bernini's hometown when the sculptor was born.

Though Bernini's life was much longer than Caravaggio's, the artists are alike in their profound influence on baroque art and their use of religious subjects for the pleasure and benefit of the Catholic Church. Bernini was an architect as well as a sculptor. He even designed the chapel housing the sculpted figure of Saint Teresa of Ávila, as the saint is in the midst of an ecstatic vision. The sculpture itself is made up of two figures: Teresa and an angelic figure that is about to pierce her heart. Teresa's expression of ecstasy has been called orgasmic by some scholars (and a few interested onlookers). The sculptor used Teresa's own descriptions of her vision as source material.

A Spanish Carmelite mystic during the Counter-Reformation, Teresa of Ávila is most well known for her writings on prayer. She was Jewish in origin, and her grandfather had been forced to confess before the Inquisition that he had been spreading Judaism. After being publicly humiliated, he moved his family to Ávila where Teresa's father was born and later Teresa herself. Teresa's writings show the influence of both Jesuit and Franciscan spirituality but also Jewish Kabbalistic mysticism.[1]

Teresa's family was pious, but her path to the convent and to spiritual encounters with God was full of fits and starts and even near-death illness. She was sick, incapacitated for several of her young years almost without explanation. Later, after writing of her spiritual experiences, she was accused of being in league with the devil. This deeply distressed her because she sought wisdom from her mentors whenever she had spiritual encounters. She wanted her experiences to be tested against the wisdom of these spiritual guides.

Teresa was affected by the Inquisition many years later when the mystical and spiritual writings she so loved were placed on the list of banned books given down by the grand inquisitor. In her distress, Christ came to her in a vision and comforted her. He said he would give her a "living book."[2]

In her autobiography called *Life*, Teresa recounts her visions and experiences with Christ. Her descriptions of God's union with her are visceral, using the metaphor of a wound. "You can't exaggerate or describe the way in which God wounds the soul," she says, "and the extreme pain this wound produces, for it causes the soul to forget itself."[3] And yet, she did her best to describe the ineffable, recounting how a beautiful angel of the Lord appeared before her with a fire-tipped golden spear.

Teresa describes her encounter with God, saying that an angel thrust a spear into her heart, puncturing her "entrails."[4] When the angel pulled the spear out again, Teresa says he "seemed to draw" her entrails out with it and left her "all on fire with a great love of God." The pain was both excruciating and yet so sweet that she "could not wish to be rid of it."[5]

Bernini's depiction of this sweet pain on the face of Teresa, as she encountered the wounding of God, could certainly be compared to an orgasm. But it also reminds me of the pain of birth, a pain that can be agonizing but also active and purposeful.

I wonder what it is like to encounter God in ecstasy. Many of the mystics have attempted to explain something that they've also called indescribable. Of course, words are inadequate to capture the whole of the experience, but they make such an encounter sound like a picture of many of the most important transitions in our lives: birth, sex, spiritual love, and death. Teresa says that the sweetness of her wounding by the Lord was something so wonderful that "the soul would wish to be always dying of this wound."[6] Death and sweetness are curled together in a terribly tender embrace.

It's a strange and uncomfortable notion to love the sweetness of God's wounding so much that the soul would die to have it. While Teresa seems to have been talking of the sweet pain of union with God, her words make me think of the little deaths we experience in life. Life is full of lesser deaths—sicknesses, moves, betrayals, losses of faith, doubts—and all of the lesser deaths, if we pay attention, can move us toward an acceptance of our own death. Sometimes death even feels preferable to the lesser deaths.

As a child and young adult, death always elicited fear in me. When I got into my midthirties, for the first time, I finally understood what it felt like to prefer death to life. One fall evening, a small trauma occurred in our little family. Neva was five when she put her arms around a friend's dog to hug him goodbye. The dog snapped and bit into her face. It happened so quickly and quietly that for a moment, I thought he'd licked her face and that when she covered up her cheek with her hands, she was just grossed out by a dog's tongue. Then I saw the blood dripping beneath her fingers.

That evening is a blur of panic. I held her in the emergency room until the doctor came, and she cried silently. The doctor and nurses strapped her down to sew up her face. I finally had to leave the room, weeping uselessly in the hallway in a nurse's arms while Matthew soothed her.

Even now, when I scroll through thousands of pictures on my computer and her swollen face comes into view from that year, I feel the creeping panic of feelings and fears.

She was okay, and she bounced back into life with the resilience of youth. I thought I was fine, too, until a week later when a panic attack hit me for the first time since I was a child. I was confused and terrified. It wasn't just the dog bite; my body had long been feeling the stress and strain of living in a struggling community, of the unexpressed expectations of motherhood and being a wife.

The night after that first panic attack, I spiraled down into an anxiety and depression that lasted a year or more.

During that year, I was in so much emotional pain that I imagined my death. I had never wanted to die before. But I imagined the end of my pain in the emotional darkness, and for a while, it looked better than life. It took time to emerge from that place, but I came out of it—just a little bit changed. What I realized later was that I had experienced a lesser death, the death of part of myself.

These kinds of deaths shake our foundations, shift our sands, tear the veil, bewilder and unmoor us. Sometimes they are deaths like a career change, a move, a breakup. Other times they are disease, trauma, abuse, or the death of a loved one.

I don't use the word *lesser* to make these deaths seem insignificant. There is nothing bigger in our lives than the effect they have on us. But they are lesser compared to *the* death. The big death that we all face.

Part of the significance of these lesser deaths I experienced—depression, anxiety, my daughter's trauma—was the realization that bad things could happen in an instant. And I didn't know what to do with that. It would take years to articulate and even begin to approach this mystery.

***

Like many of the mystics, Teresa of Ávila meditated on the passion of Christ often. In *Interior Castle*, she encourages her readers to "dwell on this mystery" of Jesus's suffering on the cross.[8] In his devotions meditating on the passion of Christ, the eighteenth-century Italian saint Alphonsus Liguori wrote that the cross of Christ reveals God's excessive love for us, both on earth and in heaven.

Saint Alphonsus also quotes Saint Francis de Sales: "'The love which is not the fruit of the Passion is feeble.'[9] . . . We can have no more pressing motive for loving God than the Passion of Jesus Christ."[10] And later, he quotes de Sales again, saying: "To know that Jesus has loved us unto death, even to the death of a Cross," should fill our hearts with a violent love.[11]

Instead of pushing death into the recesses of the human consciousness, these mystics were guided by the image of the suffering God because God's suffering taught them more about love. God knows the way our lesser deaths can leave us adrift. God know this because God experienced and suffered these kinds of deaths too.

Even in the midst of his suffering, Jesus was afflicted by fear. His journey to death on the cross was painful in many ways: it was politically humiliating (he was crucified like a criminal), personally humiliating (he was beaten and forced to carry his cross through the streets and was mocked by soldiers), and excruciating (the word *excruciating* comes from the Latin *excruciat*, or "torment," which is based on the word *cruc* or "cross"). He was even deserted by his friends. But most cruelly, God seemed to desert him too.

"My God, my God, why have you forsaken me?" Jesus cried from the cross (Matt 27:46). The relational, communal position Jesus occupied for eternity among the Trinity—begotten before all worlds—felt momentarily closed off to him. Saint Francis de Sales says that on the cross, even though he was unified with God, Jesus felt "abandoned and forsaken by his Father," and it left him in a "torrent of anguish."[12] Jesus was devastated.

If he was indeed human, "made like his brothers" and

sisters (Heb 2:17 esv), then it's reasonable to assume that the range of human fears were also part of Jesus's humanness. The gospels indicate that Jesus was plainly afraid of his death, sweating blood and asking for deliverance. But what was the nature of Jesus's fear of death? Was he afraid of the pain? The humiliation? Perhaps. But I wonder if Jesus was also afraid that God wouldn't keep God's promises. That after all of this, his death would be the end. Maybe the fear of not existing anymore is a natural part of what it means to long for survival, even for Jesus.

Those in the Middle Ages and Reformation experienced fear of death differently. Like Saint Francis de Sales in the distress of his youth, death fear was centered around the terror of hell. Would they be deemed good enough for heaven? Or were they predestined for hell anyway?

The second chapter of Hebrews explains that when Jesus died, he not only destroyed "him who holds the power of death—that is, the devil" but he also released those "who all their lives were held in slavery by their fear of death" (vv. 14–15). Like many of us do, Jesus experienced the fear of death. And then he went on ahead and conquered it.

That doesn't mean that we won't be afraid, but I wonder if what Jesus conquered was the result of this fear. The fear of death, when left unchecked, is so absorbed into the fabric of our lives that we don't even see it. And yet, we will do everything we can to maintain our structures of comfort and ease. Sometimes we will even hold up our own security and comfort above the suffering of others.

When Jesus released us from our fear of death, he was

releasing us from the compulsions inherent in the structural fear of death.[13] These compulsions to run away from death in the structures of our lives. To run from death in our refusal to admit vulnerability. To run from the ways that we have hurt others because of our fear of death.

The mystics looked hard at Jesus's death, meditating on the gruesome details and the freedom Jesus offered through his sacrifice. Jesus's death freed us to uncover our eyes. To look harder. To look again. And to ask him to help us not to be afraid anymore.

Saint Francis de Sales believed that those who lived well would not be afraid of death, echoing the influence of Reformation ideas. But he adds, "Or if you fear it, it will be with a sweet and tranquil fear, relying on the merits of the Passion of Our Lord, without which, indeed, death would be frightful and terrible to all men."[14]

This sweet fear is a little like Saint Teresa's description of the wounding of God. This terrible sweetness followed her, it was said, even after death. When Teresa of Ávila died, her body was buried without any kind of preparation. For nine months after her death, legend has it that the smell of violets, lilies, and jasmine drifted out of the place where she was buried. When the authorities decided to exhume her body to see what was happening, they found that Teresa's coffin was filled with water and earth and her clothes had disintegrated. But her body was still intact.[15] Even after being buried and exhumed twice more, the state of her body hadn't changed. Her heart and other pieces of her body were removed and given as relics to display.

I wonder if the scent of flowers was much like the sweetness of the perpetual wounds of God.

PART III

CHILDHOOD AND THE MYSTERY OF DEATH: A VICTORIAN MYSTIC

9

THE ODD VICTORIANS

In the late eighteenth century, the dying of a Scottish philosopher caused an uproar among religious folk. Throughout his work, David Hume unabashedly expressed skepticism of the afterlife. As he was on his deathbed, the religious people who had criticized him throughout his life hoped that the terror of his impending death would lead him back to faith. When his best friend, Adam Smith (the famous author of *The Wealth of Nations*), publicized the particulars of Hume's last moments, it would be a disappointment to his detractors. Smith wrote of Hume's calmness in the face of death, "depicting the philosopher telling jokes, playing cards, and conversing cheerfully with his friends."[1] Hume died peacefully, seemingly unafraid.

Hume and Smith were both philosophers of the Age of Enlightenment, a movement that began in the late seventeenth century and continued for more than a century. As in the Reformation, the strength of the individual was important to Enlightenment thinkers. An increasing distaste for the hierarchies of the Catholic Church and the monarchy sparked movements like the French Revolution, which at first glance, was concerned with liberty and equality. Eventually, the quest for the liberty of some ended up eroding the liberty of others. And by that I mean their liberty was detached because the guillotine removed their heads from their bodies. You could say that death really was the great leveler in the French Revolution—its conduit leveled off heads quite neatly.

In Europe during the Enlightenment, advances in science and medicine were providing more answers about the natural world and hope for living longer lives. Instead of just offering palliative care, deathbed medicine "became primarily interested in prolonging life."[2] But more than that, some philosophers wondered if death and disease could ultimately be eradicated through science and medicine.[3] Even the power of death itself was questioned.

The dominant beliefs about life and death were still rooted in the Christian church's ideas about God, but more Enlightenment thinkers like David Hume were beginning to wonder if death ended not in heaven or hell but in oblivion. When the individual became more important and the medical aspects of death were more widely understood, people came to fear death in a new way.[4] Author Brandy Schillace says that the combination of Enlightenment rationalism with the new focus on the self made "oblivion" even "*more* terrifying" than the imaginative terrors of hell that had gripped Catholic consciousness for centuries.[5]

It's not a surprise that a reliance on reason and the self

would lead to fear. With the secular belief in oblivion, many were also afraid at the prospect of the obliteration of this new self they'd discovered. Death is the most mysterious of human experiences. Death cannot be reasoned with—a terrifying prospect to a person who is relying on the mind's ability to work everything out.

***

In Europe, the Enlightenment tumbled into the Romantic and Victorian eras. In the pendulum swing of history, the Romantic movement emerged in late eighteenth-century Europe in reaction to the Enlightenment obsession with reason and the primacy of the mind. Romantics emphasized emotion, the purity of nature, the imagination, and individualism. They leaned back into history, looking for inspiration from a time long past when the world felt more enchanted.[6]

Where did they find creative inspiration? The medieval period. That time of horror, disease, great art, and explosive creativity. Where Reformation thinkers had prized the humanistic qualities of the classical age, of Greek and Roman antiquity, Romantic artists yearned for the Middle Ages. They felt stifled by the Enlightenment preoccupation with reason, so they created emotionally stirring, dramatic, idealized images of knights and beautiful women. They produced writing that was reminiscent of Dante's *Divine Comedy*. To Romantic thinkers and artists, the medieval period represented a time when the world was more apt to hold space for the mysterious, for the fantastical, and for the unknowable.

Something unknowable like death can bring a mixture

of terror and hope, even if that hope remains unfulfilled. A teenage Mary Wollstonecraft Shelley wrote a novel in 1818 (right in the middle of the Romantic era) that set the stage for science fiction and modern horror. In many ways, Mary and her married lover Percy Shelley embodied the artistic expressions of the Romantic era: it is said that they fell in love while reading her parent's writing (her mother was the feminist author Mary Wollstonecraft) and lying across her dead mother's grave.[7] How very medieval of them.

Mary began her novel *Frankenstein* as a ghost story, written on a getaway with Percy and the famous Romantic antihero Lord Byron. She was nursing her second child at the time, after having lost her first baby only weeks after birth. She was pregnant with her third child by the time the novel was completed.

Some of the themes in *Frankenstein* mirror the unknown progress of science and death during the Romantic and Victorian eras. The concerns of the eponymous Victor Frankenstein, the scientist who creates the unnamed monster of the novel, reflect the question that the medical community was asking: Could they possess power over death?

The novel also seems to bleed with Mary Shelley's personal grief and horror: only one of her four children survived long past birth. In the midst of profound loss, both Mary and Percy Shelley found themselves believing that the dead could be revived.[8]

From the distance of centuries, their deep hope in something that, to us, looks hopeless is heartbreaking. But death brings out hopes, whether they are hopes for the resuscitation of a child who has died or, for Christians, the hope for final resurrection.

For the medical community of these eras, the reversal of death had a lot more to do with science than with faith. When people began to hope that it might actually be possible to reverse death, mortality became a space where grief and mourning might be prolonged. Maybe this is one of the reasons why the Victorians had such an odd fixation on death.

***

The Victorian era began when a young Queen Victoria took the throne in the middle of the nineteenth century, during a period of great progress and social change. Perhaps it was because of this mix of social progress along with a culture that was confused and curious that death became a fixation for Victorians. They would cope with the prevalence of death in the ways that only a buttoned-up, inventive, and inquisitive culture could. This era held together such inventions and advancements as the telegraph, the modern railway, widespread use of vaccinations, abolishment of slavery, and Darwin's publication of *On the Origin of Species*, alongside the rise of spiritualism and the use of mediums to connect with the dead. Within a culture that seemed to be finding more answers to existential questions, there was still a deep longing for mystery.

Though Britain was living in the glorious aftermath of Enlightenment advances in science and industry, enjoying all of the betterment that such progress could offer, vast discrepancies still existed between the lives of the wealthy and the poor. As ever, the most vulnerable often paid the heaviest price. The Industrial Revolution opened up more work opportunities, but many of the worst jobs went to children, especially poor children, who began working as early as eight years old.

As opposed to their Romantic counterparts, Victorian artists were often more realistic than melodramatic about the underbelly of life in Britain and Europe. Charles Dickens brilliantly depicted the bleakness of a life in poverty—the workhouse and debtors' prison—in books like *Oliver Twist*, *Little Dorrit*, and the aptly named *Bleak House* (which depicts the bleakness of the rich as well as the poor). Workhouses were government-run facilities for those who couldn't pay their debts. Some of Dickens's most memorable characters, like Oliver Twist, the Artful Dodger, Pip, or Ebenezer Scrooge, are those who have learned how to survive or find hope and redemption despite a culture that seems intent on beating them down by poverty, cruelty, or suffering.

Dickens's novel *Little Dorrit* is the tale of Amy Dorrit, a young woman who is born and raised in a debtors' prison in London called Marshalsea. Dorrit's father is so destitute that she grows up within the walls of the prison, finding a sort of community in conditions that were often wretched and filthy. Dickens's novel satirizes and skewers the cruelty of society that would force its most vulnerable into such conditions. Amy Dorrit's experience was close to his heart: his own father had been sent to Marshalsea when Charles Dickens was twelve for a small debt to a baker. Charles Dickens was forced to work in a shoe-polish factory to help support his family.

Those who inhabited these workhouses and prisons

were vulnerable to the overreach of the eager scientific community. In the earlier decades of the nineteenth century and even before that, body dissection and anatomy became important with the expanding knowledge of medicine. Executed criminals had been used for dissection, sometimes publicly, but when executions declined, a black-market trade in corpses developed, including grave robbing.

With the Anatomy Act of 1832—meant to stem the distasteful practice of grave robbing—the Brits were attempting to be more civilized in their handling of corpses. But doctors were now *legally* allowed to use the unclaimed corpses of the workhouse poor along with the bodies of the executed for dissection. Those with business acumen, as always, found a way to make this work in their favor. The people who ran workhouses made their own trade in selling the corpses of those who died without family and whose bodies were never claimed. In the most tragic cases, those who were totally destitute resorted to selling their own family members to "corpse dealers" who intentionally set up shop in economically depressed parts of the city.[9]

Those with power and wealth were the ones making the laws *and* doing the dissecting in the name of science. It wasn't their loved ones' bodies that were being exploited and anatomized. The poor had every reason to be suspicious of the imbalance of power.

Dissection photographs still exist from this era. Some of them show the increased callousness of young students studying anatomy. These students arranged human cadavers in artistic ways as well as ways that were obviously meant to evoke laughter: smiling students holding up the heads of corpses, bodies placed in "humorous" scenarios like poker games. The photographs are reminiscent of the 1980s movie *Weekend at Bernie's*, where two fumbling twentysomethings pretend that the eponymous Bernie is alive, propping him up throughout the movie in increasingly hilarious situations. But mockery of bodies in a movie comedy is different than the abuse of dead bodies under the guise of science, particularly when those bodies were provided by the most vulnerable in society.[10]

A decade after the Anatomy Act, a fury erupted among working-class people. They were terrified that vivisepulture, or the act of burying people alive, was being used as a discipline for people in workhouses. I wouldn't blame them for thinking so. They saw evidence all the time that the poorest in society were vulnerable to all kinds of abuse. And in the midst of this panic, doctors weren't a lot of help. History professor George K. Behlmer says that Victorian doctors were "often confused, sometimes careless, and . . . occasionally cruel . . . poorly positioned to reassure the public about their ability to know death when they saw it." What's more, "No one test for death, other than the slow and unpleasant wait for putrefaction, was regarded as definitive by itself."[11] A medical community that was supposed to bring "enlightenment" and knowledge often exacerbated the problem.

***

For all their advances in medicine, doctors couldn't stop early death from epidemics like typhus and cholera. The Victorian fixation on death was shaped not only by this prevalence of death but also by Queen Victoria, whose unique behaviors influenced mourning practices for generations after. When Victoria's beloved husband, Albert, died at the young age of forty-two, she began to dress in the black mourning clothes that would define both her individual look and Victorian mourning customs. Victoria's look "ushered in a strict code" that gave fashion protocols for the first and second year of mourning with variations to clothing in subsequent mourning years. The codes ranged from "secondary" to "ordinary" to "half mourning" when various colors were allowed to add contrast to the full black.[12]

Queen Victoria might've been onto something with those mourning clothes. When a culture doesn't allow for long periods of grief and the mourner is expected to jump right back into life, a visual statement reminding a community that we have been changed by grief or tragedy might be a relief.[13]

Of course, things can always be taken too far. When fashion becomes coded, what begins as a way to show grief can become something else. Mourning fashion was enforced even with those who might not actually be mourning, like a young widow forced into a loveless marriage to a much older man by the need to make an advantageous match. One such widow decided that her activities didn't have to be limited by her black clothing. So she took her mourning to the seaside and started a fashion trend of black swimwear.[14]

Mourning wear also became increasingly expensive and decadent, a terrible hardship for the many people in poverty in Victorian England. Eventually Victoria herself was forced to discourage such excess.

Queen Victoria kept her husband's daily rituals for

years after his death, going so far as to have servants bring in his clothes every morning and clean out his chamber pot and linens. She withdrew from public life for ten years. After a decade of seclusion, the political sphere grew restless and the public began to question Victoria's mental health. Eventually, she came out of hiding, but she still insisted on wearing her "widow's weeds" until her death decades later.

***

The Queen wasn't the only one of her era to struggle with letting go of a dead loved one. Another custom, a Victorian version of memento mori, revealed a lot about the approach to death in nineteenth-century Britain: photography of the dead.

This kind of photography was quite different from the mockery of cadavers by Victorian students of anatomy. In the 1840s and '50s, new camera technology called the daguerreotype was in its heyday. Family portraiture was a luxury that had only been accessible to the wealthy who could pay to sit for hours in front of a portrait painter. With the invention of these photographic portraits, more households had access to family pictures. But the process was still expensive and time-consuming. It wasn't, therefore, unusual, for a person to be in a portrait only once. And sometimes, the only portrait of a person or a family was done after one or more of the members had died.[15]

Though these photographs seem to be a type of memento mori, author Brandy Schillace points out that a particular aspect of the portraiture may cause us to wonder if the purpose was truly to help one "remember your death." In these Victorian family portraits, not only were the dead pictured but they were often posed *as if they hadn't died.* A portrait of five of a family's children would include a deceased child propped up beside her siblings as if she were still alive. While some of the individuals pictured are clearly dead, in other portraits you might not realize that there is a dead body if you didn't know already.[16]

Was this an effort to remember the dead or is it a denial of death? The Victorians, like those in the medieval era, had peculiar and often disturbing approaches to death. As with every era, we are often confused in the ways we approach death. We try to cope with death in good ways as well as in destructive and unhealthy ways. It might be difficult for us to understand why a society with so many advances would resort to such strange death habits. Though we might also consider why a society like ours, with even more advancements in science, medicine, and psychology, might find itself grief-challenged (but that's a question for another chapter).

10

AN ARTISTIC SENSE FOR DEATH

In the final decade of the seventeenth century, back when the Enlightenment was just beginning, a small massacre took place in the Scottish Highlands; it was so brutal that news of its horrors reached down into the heart of Britain, even to city dwellers who were far removed from the inner workings of clan loyalties.

Clan Campbell had sworn loyalty to a new monarch, King William of Orange. They were now his soldiers, tasked with enforcing his rule against the other clans who had not claimed loyalty to the new king. The Campbells' neighbors, Clan MacDonald, were still under a sworn oath to King William's father-in-law, James II, when word reached them in 1692 that King William expected their loyalty. The MacDonalds sent a letter to the authorities, hoping to change their loyalties before a crucial date.

But the inclement winter weather blocked passes through the Highlands and slowed the letter's journey. In the meantime, Clan Campbell showed up at Clan Mac-

Donald's doorstep waiting for the set-upon date when it would be too late for the MacDonalds to throw their weight behind William. In true Clan fashion, while the Campbell soldiers waited for their orders, the MacDonalds showed generous hospitality to them for nearly two weeks, playing games and eating together.

Unfortunately, whether through sabotage or just bad luck, the MacDonalds' letter of loyalty failed to reach William's desk on time. Orders were sent for the Campbells, upon pain of death, to "fall upon the rebels, the MacDonalds of Glencoe, and to put all to the sword under seventy."[1] The early-morning massacre devastated Clan MacDonald. Forty of their number were killed, even the clan chief who, it is said, was caught unawares in the act of replenishing his guests' whisky to send them on their way.[2]

Those of Clan MacDonald who escaped were to face exposure and starvation in the bitter winter weather as they fled to nearby caves. Many more died. Of the survivors was an infant named Ronald MacDonald, who made it to a small fishing village in the north. His descendants would face more battles, trials, and massacres. But his great-great-great grandson would put all of the hardships and beauty of his place and the trauma of his ancestors into spiritual words, stories, sermons, and family plays that would thrill and influence generations of other storytellers. He would become a beloved author, poet, preacher, and mystical thinker of Victorian Britain.

His name was George MacDonald.

Though he was born in the mid-nineteenth century into a household with some Calvinist influences, the Celtic traditions and faiths of his Highland ancestors still thrummed in George MacDonald's spirit. His grandfather spoke Gaelic, his great-grandfather was Catholic-born but later became a Presbyterian, his grandmother was an "Independent church rebel," and his mother's brother was a "Gaelic-speaking radical."[3] In George MacDonald, these disparate religious affiliations and belief systems had been gathered. From the stodgiest of village churches, to the city cathedrals, to a faith so ancient it seemed to emerge out of the very stones and hills, the melding of traditions and faiths were part of the imaginative landscape of George MacDonald's childhood.

Though the massacre of Clan MacDonald had scattered his ancestors long ago, still, that "fey streak" from his Celtic family history bloomed into "a fully elaborated mysticism" in George MacDonald.[4] In that ancestry, George MacDonald held the tensions of the Reformation and Counter-Reformation. But he also was a product of the tensions between other movements and eras: the Enlightenment of the eighteenth century and the Romantic and Victorian eras of the nineteenth century.

***

A German Romantic who went by the pen name Novalis had a great impact on the Victorian Romantic George MacDonald. Novalis's short life and work fit the cliché image of the melancholy Romantic artist: he was a sad poet whose work was infused with the loss of his very young fiancée, Sophie; he was an afflicted genius who died young and left behind a body of work that was published posthumously. Novalis was also a mystic, fixating on death and longing. When his fiancée died, his mystical leanings became more pronounced. His grief swept him into the spiritual world, into meditations on Sophie, into meditations on death.

Novalis believed that the classical period, after which so many of the Enlightenment thinkers had hungered, "held a deep terror of death" because of its rationalistic fixation on the "here and now." Christianity, on the other hand, had offered an alternative to the fear of death. The resurrection of Christ had defeated death and "reconciled the world to the idea of death."[5] Fellow German Romantic Friedrich Schlegel told Novalis that he had an "artistic sense for death."[6] It was this sense of the "good death" that drew George MacDonald to Novalis and inspired much of MacDonald's writing.[7] Novalis offered MacDonald unique inspiration for ideas about childhood, myth, and what a good fairy tale is.[8]

George MacDonald was influenced by Romantic artists like Novalis but also by Victorian sensibilities. His life span was nestled inside the Victorian era, a time that began just about a decade after he was born and ended with Queen Victoria's death, a mere four years before MacDonald's own in 1905. MacDonald would offer a mystical sort of insight to the Victorians and their unique and odd views about death.

11

UNLOCKING THE IMPRISONED MIND

My Church of Christ upbringing, though not Arminian and not Reformed like the Enlightenment Calvinism that George MacDonald and Saint Francis de Sales wrestled with, was a byproduct of the same rationalism. Begun by Presbyterian ministers in the nineteenth century, the movement aimed to restore the church to the purity of the first-century church as described in the apostle Paul's epistles. The founding ministers believed that if everyone read the Bible without denominational creeds, interpretation would be uniform and therefore unifying. These intellectual and theological men were doing a sort of Martin Luther–lite: reforming the problems they saw in the institutional church. In other words, by studying the Bible and looking at the first-century churches, my tradition was searching for the correct way of being a Christian and doing church.

In my childhood, when deciding whether a contemporary question could find its answer in the Bible, it was not unusual to hear: "Speak where the Bible speaks and stay silent where the Bible stays silent." My tradition valued Scripture and the church very highly. This knowledge of the Bible was a gift to me. I knew the Bible well. I memorized verses, built replicas of the temple from the Old Testament, and won awards in Bible tournaments, where we answered trivia questions about books of the Bible. I could read Scripture at competitions, even if I wasn't allowed to do so during worship because I was a girl. My tradition practiced believer's baptism and most kids could sing in four-part harmony by late elementary school.

As I grew up, though, I was pestered by a certain feeling when it came to church. It was the same feeling I had when I was assigned *The Pilgrim's Progress* in my high school English class: both my childhood faith and John Bunyan's classic book felt stagnant. If the life of faith is a farm, it began to look to me like a yellowed field. There was nothing to give it life and bright colors. My faith felt dormant and a little boring.

I decided to move to Scotland for graduate school for very emotional reasons. I had been to Scotland as a young adult and experienced the stirrings of something very old and mystical in the land—a kinship, a fantasy, a feeling that just around that gravestone or that tree could be the doorway to another world. I felt the way I always did when I read novels like the Lord of the Rings trilogy.

Scotland and those fantasy novels evoked in me a deep longing for something that was missing. I didn't realize it at the time, but now I can see that the influence of my church tradition on my faith had only left a tiny gap for mystery. I was desperate to step through and let the mystery in.

The first time I lugged my suitcases up the stairs of my flat on the East Sands on the North Sea of St. Andrews in Scotland, it was early September. The flat I would share with three other women my first year was housed in a concrete block of a building that looked like it had been built to withstand bombs in World War II. Or maybe it was just the wild winds that blew off the North Sea that needed to be fortified against, separated from the beach by a gray stone wall.

The inside of the flat wasn't much newer: the carpets were probably from the 1960s, the bathroom had stains only dorm bathrooms could have, the kitchen was tight, and I'm not sure any of us ever thought to divvy up cleaning duties.

My single bed was shoved up against a concrete wall that happened to also be the outer wall of the building. The only heat came from a pitiful radiator that sometimes kept half the room warm. I was from Texas, so I had to depend on my Scottish roommate to help me learn how to survive nights that seemed unendingly chilled. I learned early on what a hot water bottle was, and I also learned what it felt like to wake up to a third-degree burn on my ankle from an improperly used water bottle.

The windy chill made me feel a kinship to the British writers I'd studied and romanticized in my undergraduate years like George Eliot, Jane Austen, and the Brontë sisters, who were often pictured suffering through cold nights, writing in fingerless gloves and shawls. Oh, brother. Living in Scotland obviously suited my natural melancholy just fine, or perhaps it indulged it rather terribly. It was a privilege to live here, romantic to live on the beach even if it was always too cold to swim. Only the bravest—or perhaps the foolhardiest—dared.

When I arrived that first September, the days were still long. But a few months later, the night took its palms to the sunlight and squeezed it together so that, in late December, our daylight was as short as eight hours. The sun would rise around nine o'clock and set at about four o'clock—just about the time school hours kept us inside. You wouldn't be a student long before you heard about the necessity of SAD lamps that could clip on caps or desks, accompanying you during long study hours, pumping Vitamin D into your sallow skin, staving off the depression.

Inside that cold dorm room, at the edge of the village of St. Andrews, the sunlight of my Texas home far away, I would lie awake shivering against the wall and wondering what I believed anymore.

The school of theology where I studied was a ten-minute walk along a path above the beach into town. When I started my degree, I began learning all sorts of different theological ways of thinking, not just in my classes but from my classmates. One friend taught me about icons, and that, contrary to the things I'd heard from Christians who were afraid of Catholicism, most people didn't worship them. Another taught me about social justice and introduced me to liberation theology. Some friends brought me to their Episcopal church where I fell in love with the full sensual experience of liturgical worship.

Still more friends were studying George MacDonald and his influence on writers like Tolkien and C. S. Lewis.

I felt an affinity with MacDonald, particularly when I realized that MacDonald's love of the imagination and fantasy were part of a longing to recapture mystery in the terrain of a rational Christianity.

Perhaps authors like MacDonald who built rich fantasy and fairy worlds are similar to the mystics, offering up a longing for something beyond and a comfort with mystery. The mystics, with their visions and angst and transformed lives, their touches of joy and grace, seek God even in the not-yet messiness of life and in the mystery of death.

The Enlightenment had not encouraged mystery. Maybe the triumph of science and reason, even as it influenced the doctrine of the church, was specifically a triumph (if only momentary) of reason and logic *over and against* many of the things that mark a mystical life: an openness and a seeking of that which cannot be worked out with reason.

Much of the mystical language that emerged out of the Enlightenment was from artists: writers, poets, and painters who took stock of the revolutions happening around the Western world and wondered at their significance. This shouldn't be too surprising. Art and mysticism have some things in common.

Art can offer to the world what mysticism offers to religious institutions: a new lens through which to look at what we've become accustomed to passing by every day without thinking twice. Just as the mystical sight can help us see our piety and religion anew, poetry can look at a flower and give it new life by describing its patterns, connecting those patterns to other things through metaphor, and resurrecting its awe in our vision.

Romantic poets like William Blake, Percy Shelley, Lord Byron, William Wordsworth, and Samuel Taylor Coleridge believed in the primacy of art and the imagination in seeking true reality. These ideas would profoundly influence George MacDonald. It was Coleridge who realized, as poet Malcolm Guite notes, that the Enlightenment had "constructed *a prison of the mind* and that the imagination, as an agent both of perception and renewal might at last unlock it—a golden key."[1] Guite says that Coleridge fought to unlock the imprisoned mind and then gave that "key" to George MacDonald.

MacDonald penned a short story called "The Golden Key," a peculiar and beautiful fairy tale that deals with death and the imagination profoundly. In "The Golden Key," a girl and boy named Tangle and Mossy find themselves lost and wandering through fairyland, with all of its uncanny rhythms and strange ways. A godlike figure named Grandmother gathers the two lost children up into the haven of her home, offering them her mystical rest and wisdom. The she sends them out into the wilds of fairyland on a lifelong spiritual journey.

They trek through hazards, dangerous peaks, and a glassy plain where shadows reflect such beautiful figures and scenes that Mossy and Tangle repeatedly long "after the country whence the shadows came."[2]

They meet and are cared for by three spiritual figures, all of them called "Old Man," but, in truth, they are varying stages of youth; the oldest and indeed wisest of the men is only a child playing with toys on a bed of moss. In Mossy's old age, he encounters the Old Man of the Sea who sends him to bathe. The cleansing renews Mossy so that his wrinkles and gray hair have vanished and his feet no longer ache.

The Old Man says to Mossy: "You have tasted of death now. . . . Is it good?"

Mossy replies: "It is good. . . . It is better than life."

"No," says the Old Man. "It is only more life."[3]

Tangle and Mossy's journey is a marriage of two people who go through life together. But their journey, particularly Tangle's individual one, also has elements of the mystical life of faith. It is upon death that Tangle is transformed by the encounters with three figures who represent "essential phases in spiritual growth"—her senses are illuminated variously by water and fire so that she can see and hear in ways that have nothing to do with her eyes and ears.[4]

She is, in a sense, awakened by death.

MacDonald's writings are full of this rich combination of mystery, fantasy, and the theology of death. But even with all the beauty in his crafting of stories, what is equally touching is the way that George MacDonald lived his life. He approached the deaths in his life with even more tenderness than he exhibited in his art.

When I heard George MacDonald scholar Kirstin Jeffrey Johnson give a talk recently, she spoke about his life as if everything he did was fueled by his radical hospitality.[5] George MacDonald and his wife, Louisa, along with their eleven children and several foster children, put on performances of their personal adaptations of classic works. And, in radical fashion, they invited everyone.

In the class structure of British Victorian society, the poor and the lower classes didn't generally mix with upper classes, particularly in the home. But MacDonald's family rebelled against these class distinctions, inviting both "paupers and princesses" to their family picnics.[6] Theater and plays were considered low society and scandalous to watch, much less for Christians to perform. In response to scandal, the MacDonald family put on a production of *The Pilgrim's Progress*, the most beloved of Christian writings. They good-naturedly tempted stuffy Christians to criticize or come and watch what they were doing. The MacDonalds took their plays on the road, traveling as an acting troupe and performing in public halls in both England and Scotland.

The home of the MacDonald family was a place where many were welcomed for respite. Numerous letters to members of the MacDonald family thank them for hosting: famous writers, mothers who needed a break, artists, and friends who were treated like family. The hospitality of the MacDonalds was so generous that when the family had to move to Italy to stabilize George MacDonald's failing health, their Victorian friends pooled their money and built them a house large enough to continue hosting both local Italian peasants and the highborn in poetry readings and plays. It was like a GoFundMe, Victorian-style.[7]

Perhaps it was because George MacDonald knew suffering that he was able to offer respite for those who were suffering too. MacDonald was deeply acquainted with grief. His mother died when he was six, and three of his siblings died before him. But most tragic of all, he and Louisa survived four of their eleven children, who died of tuberculosis over the course of many years.

MacDonald's poems from his collection *A Book of Strife in the Form of the Diary of an Old Soul* seem to be motivated by this struggle, the unimaginable grief of the loss of his children. In one poem, he writes both of the equalizing power of death and the hope that death will reunite him with his children:

> Death, like high faith, levelling, lifteth all.
> When I awake, my daughter and my son,
> Grown sister and brother, in my arms shall fall.[8]

These poems are also filled with his anguish and the internal struggle of grief in the midst of his faith.

> I cannot see, my God, a reason why
> From morn to night I go not gladsome, free;
> For, if thou art what my soul thinketh thee,
> There is no burden but should lightly lie.[9]

Poems like these, though they emerge from a deep well of sorrow, are infused with hope. They express a longing for the renewal, reconciliation, and reunion that heaven and the new creation will bring. Like his poems, MacDonald held the ache of loss with hope through numerous letters he wrote to people who were grieving. He often sent letters of condolence weeks after the fact of death because he knew that "a time comes, worse than the first" when those who were mourning a loss would encounter more waves of grief.[10] In a letter to a young woman who lost a loved one, he begins his poignant correspondence with "Let my heart come near to yours, and talk a little bit to it."[11]

MacDonald's letters are filled with both a profound understanding of the mourner's grief, compassion for their loss, and an imaginative picture of the hope of the afterlife. For MacDonald, the "very notion of heaven" is to "have all we love with us" in a "homely" place where we will "talk of all the old times with the hearts of divinely glad little ones" and "feel our bodies as free, as little held down and oppressed."[12]

His letters recall the compassion and gentleness of Saint Francis de Sales, who also wrote letters of condolence to those who mourned. Like de Sales, MacDonald had an aversion to what he saw as the harsh theology of the Calvinists, whose doctrines seemed to leave little room for joy, artistic expression, and compassion. In some ways, John Bunyan's classic work *The Pilgrim's Progress*, the tales of a man and woman (Christian and Christiana) who represent every person's journey through the joys and spiritual perils of life, embodies the stodginess of Enlightenment rationalism. But MacDonald saw something more in Bunyan's story. Or perhaps he was able to draw out the best of Bunyan.

In their performances of *The Pilgrim's Progress*, the MacDonalds brought mystery to rationalism. MacDonald shared Bunyan's view of God's redemption, embraced the mythic quality of Bunyan's allegorical tale, and infused it with mystery. His novels reflect this engagement with myth and mystery and the imagination. Through story, the imagination, and radical hospitality, MacDonald offered an antidote to Enlightenment and Victorian rationalism that had pervaded Christianity since the Reformation. He sought to reconnect with mystery through myth.[13]

Mystery is something our culture (even sometimes our Western Christian culture) tends to ignore until we are faced with hard stuff like death and decay and suffering. When these things arrive on our doorsteps, our response to them often reveals how much we have been uncomfortable with mystery. Maybe we are unprepared. And our lack of preparation, our lack of training in mystery, leaves us with truncated grief or questions too enormous for a stagnant theology to handle.

MacDonald's works served as a corrective to his readers who were wedged so tightly in a faith of the mind, offering more mythical encounters with God. His writings have helped me and generations of readers see that faith in God isn't about thinking our way into heaven with fear, severity, and a reasonable mind. In MacDonald's story, God is a wise embodied being who rescues and comforts, who teaches and nudges us toward the things we fear, who welcomes us into a safe haven. In MacDonald's world, God is mysterious and loving.

Still, mystery isn't always comfortable. Sometimes it is painful. What MacDonald did in his life, he also did in his writing: he offered stories that can help us deal with the realities of life and death.

12

THE COURAGE OF FAIRY

Even though I didn't really understand it, I loved George MacDonald's "The Golden Key" when I first read it in graduate school. I love it even more now after age and subsequent reads. I'm not sure I will ever fully understand it, but I've felt more grief and experienced the not-yetness of life so that, when I reread the story years later, Tangle and Mossy's longing for the place of shadows is much more poignant. The beauty of MacDonald's stories, and really the beauty of any good story, is both its timelessness and its agelessness. Surprisingly, my children loved it too when I read it to them for the first time. It's an odd sort of story, and it doesn't always make immediate sense. My children begged me to keep reading anyway.

George MacDonald was inspired to write his fairy tales by other stories that had timeless resonance, like the folktales, myths, and stories that nearly every community has spoken to one another for millennia. Traditionally, fairy tales, even if they were told to children, were taken seriously by all members of a community. These tales taught truths that had been gleaned from a culture's history, from their wars and times of peace, from their surviving, thriving, and dying. These communal stories taught the most elemental truths about life. As Madeleine L'Engle wrote in *Walking on Water*,

> This questioning of the meaning of being, and dying and being, is behind the telling of stories around tribal fires at night; behind the drawing of animals on the walls of caves; the singing of melodies of love in spring, and of the death of green in autumn. It is part of the deepest longing of the human psyche, a recurrent ache in the hearts of all God's creatures.[1]

Though these kinds of stories weren't specifically told to children, children were in attendance, doing the good work of listening and learning to the communal lessons inherent in these tales.[2]

The way stories are told or written for children in every culture is a marker of the way children are viewed in their own time. The state of a child's soul has agonized theologians and philosophers for centuries. It was Augustine who first posited the doctrine of original sin in the fourth century, that children were born into the world with souls already tainted. The Catholic Church would officially adopt this doctrine during the sixteenth-century Councils of Trent.

In the seventeenth century, MacDonald's beloved author John Bunyan, who also believed that all people were born into sin, only wrote things for children for a moral purpose. MacDonald scholar Daniel Gabelman says that Bunyan "condescended to childish rhyming only in order to save children's souls from the webs, traps, and snares of childish games and toys."[3]

Educated Enlightenment thinkers and theologians like Bunyan both, for different reasons, viewed fairy tales and fantasy literature as improper for children.[4] In the eighteenth century, philosopher Jean-Jacques Rousseau's novel *Emile* challenged the doctrine of original sin. Rousseau posited that children were, instead, born innocent and "completely in accord with nature." If they were taught "selfishness, cruelty and perversity" as they matured, it wasn't the sinful world but the damaging influence of "oppressive institutions like governments, schools, churches, and businesses" that were to blame.[5] In turn, Rousseau believed that children shouldn't be given books because they were a corrupting influence whose "seeds of innumerable cultural weeds . . . might at any moment sprout in the child's isolated and carefully guarded Eden."[6]

For all of his moral posturing, Rousseau sent his own five children to a foundling hospital for abandoned babies, believing they would be better off as wards of the state since he couldn't pay for their education. So much for avoiding the stain of the world's institutions. Maybe he was just too caught up in his ideals to do the actual hard work of parenting.

When the nineteenth century gave way to the Romantic era, childhood became a dreamy place for Romantic artists, when God was closest to the individual, where goodness was strongest. In the Victorian era, childhood (at least middle- and upper-class childhood) was celebrated and fawned over so much that some adults even longed to return to childhood themselves.[7] Victorian authors like Lewis Carroll (who was friends with George MacDonald) were offended by the Bunyan belief in the necessity of moralistic teaching. Carroll believed that any moral teaching should be avoided so that "adult sophistication" wouldn't taint a child's innocent imagination.[8]

When Lewis Carroll sent a moralistic children's book to George MacDonald's daughter Lilia, he wrote somewhat humorously, "the book is intended for you to look at the outside, and then put it away in the bookcase: the *inside* is not meant to be read."[9] Carroll brought his disgust of moralism into his famous *Alice in Wonderland* books, having various villainous or silly characters lecture on and on about the goodness of moral teaching.[10]

Both views of childhood, whether Bunyan's didacticism or Carroll's Romantic/Victorian view of the ills of the moralistic tradition, had something in common: anxiety. Childhood was seen as "fragile and easily combustible . . . full of anxiety about stories for children."[11]

There is still quite a bit of anxiety about our children and the stories we tell them. Contemporary scientists and psychologists have focused a lot of energy on children and childhood, giving us a deeper understanding of their psychological needs, how they thrive and grow, how we can teach them to become compassionate adults. All of this expert knowledge has encouraged us to be more attuned to our children's inner lives. The publishing industry has responded to the emphasis we place on childhood: what used to be a small genre has become one of the most financially viable genres of literature. There are books for children and young adults on nearly every topic.

On the other hand, this focus on childhood can have its downsides. Parents are prone to the anxiety of cultural pressure. And the pressure starts in utero: pregnant mothers are told what we should eat or not, how much weight to gain or not, what vitamins to take, what music to listen to, how much to exercise. When our babies are born, we are commanded to breastfeed and then we're told not to let them cry or they won't attach properly. Simultaneously, we ought to let them cry it out or they will be spoiled. We have to feed them only good and wholesome things. As they grow, we are supposed to read to them every night or they won't be good readers, put them in sports leagues in kindergarten or they won't get onto the team in high school. They have to thrive socially by having every opportunity in athletics, music, and academics.

Maybe we can (literally) take a page from George MacDonald's book as well as his family life when it comes to the way we see childhood and how we tell stories to children. While MacDonald has elements of a Romantic view of childhood in some of his stories, his close relationship with his eleven children and his deep faith in God gave him a more measured view.

MacDonald explains that he didn't consider himself to strictly be writing for children: "[I] write . . . for the childlike, whether of five, or fifty, or seventy-five."[12] Just like those stories told to all ages around campfires, *all* were welcome in the world of fairy. MacDonald certainly hoped that his stories would teach something good, but he shied away from the didacticism that had defined the Enlightenment-influenced stories of his youth. And MacDonald's welcoming writing was consistent with the way he and his family lived: all were welcome to the plays his family performed, to the stories they told in community.

MacDonald's stories had their source in his love of fairy tales, but ultimately, they came from his love of the Bible and the rich world built in those stories. Not only is the Old Testament full of strange, troubling, confusing, and beautiful tales, but Jesus himself also preached through story. My husband once said in a sermon that in his last days on earth, Jesus could've made everything clear for his followers. He could've told them the secrets of the kingdom, explained exactly how and why he would die and be resurrected. He could've told them the deep mysteries of the universe. Instead, in the middle chapters of Luke, as Jesus makes his way to Jerusalem to die, he tells parables. Ten chapters of stories.

Jesus knew that transformation doesn't come through doctrine. It comes through stories. Stories that surprise. Stories that comfort. Stories that disturb. Stories that sit with us, baffle us, plague us, and move us, even thousands of years later.

But the meaning of these stories is often most evident in their communal telling. As far as I see it, one way to teach children about darker subjects, about lessons of life and death, is telling stories in community. The stories we cater only to them and their stage of development can miss larger questions that are asked on a communal level. We no longer have as many "communal campfires" for storytelling that provide cohesive understandings and questions of "the meaning of being, and dying and being," as L'Engle says. In our efforts to focus on their stages of growth, our children's access to communal storytelling, where children would sit with their parents and grandparents, with people of all ages and hear the same tales, has lessened.

One of the places this communal storytelling still happens is in our churches. Churchgoers come together every week to retell the same story, over and over: the story of God's relationship with creation, the story of a love so deep that God became incarnate and died in order to be with us. This glorious story is often gruesome, full of blood and pain and suffering.

Still, we sometimes resist the complexities in these communal stories—stories about David and Goliath, Noah's ark, and the Exodus—when we sanitize them into happy retellings of nuanced Bible stories. If we need to tell them more simply for the very young, that's fine. But what do we do as our children grow if we have ignored the parts of the story that we find problematic or disturbing? Years later, they will look back on those stories and see the real truth and might feel betrayed. Madeleine L'Engle says that children should be given "the whole Bible, uncut, taking out none of the sex, none of the violence, knowing that the Bible balances itself and that they will do their own automatic deleting."[13]

Author Amy Peterson talks about reading difficult biblical stories to her children at night in her book *Where Goodness Still Grows*. She says, "We don't skip any of the stories, and I don't pretend to have all the answers to the questions they raise. Children know when a story has been cleaned up for their sake. They can also appreciate a story that can't be explained."[14]

Amy is right: children *do* know. And that's another thing that MacDonald understood and emphasized about childlikeness. Philosophers and theologians have been so concerned for centuries about the soul or spirit or intellect of children. But what about *our* souls and intellects and spirits? Can the childlike approach to our biggest existential questions offer something to adults too?

Psychiatrist Robert Coles, who has spent many years working with children, says that their questions about death are a lot more sophisticated than we often give them credit for: "The questions Tolstoy asked . . . ('Where Do We Come From? What Are We? Where Are We Going?'), are eternal questions children ask more intensely, unremittingly, and subtly than we sometimes imagine."[15]

I know this is true with my own children. Neva's comments about death when we sat on the tilted bench in the child's cemetery in our Illinois community took me by surprise. Jude has asked pointed questions about death that other people might not have the courage to ask. Many parents can attest to the first stuttering shock of a child's sophisticated questions about where children go when they die or whether grandma will be scared in her coffin underground. Children often have a sort of bravery that adults can lose as they face the pain of the world and the reality of death. This courage was part of MacDonald's philosophy. Childhood, and particularly childlikeness, was to MacDonald "fearlessness, or at least bravery in the face of fear."[16]

MacDonald wrote for the "childlike" not because he idolized childhood. By writing of a fairy world that showed a true reality, he wanted to recapture the childlike in all of us, to inflame our imaginative and moral spirits. He invited each of us, whether we are five, or fifty, or seventy-five to "enter fearlessly into his beneficently beautiful world of once-upon-a-time," where we may find the courage that can save us.[17] Facing our fear of death takes the courage of fairy, a courage that for children is "the most natural thing in the world."[18]

13

FALLING FROM A DINOSAUR

One fall when we were living in the farming community in Illinois, Matthew was ready to butcher the two-dozen geese that lived in our strawberry fields all season, weeding and otherwise creating a lot of noise and chaos. Neva and Jude, who were five and three, wanted to follow their father out to the machine shop on that cold morning to watch. But I was hesitant. I wondered if it would be good for them to witness the death and defeathering of the geese they'd helped raise from goslings in our basement. Neva, whose scars from her dog bite were still pink, was particularly eager. So I sent them out anyway.

When I went to check on them later, I found Jude standing stiffly at the door to the shop, his eyes wide. He had red splatters of blood on his pants.

"I don't want to stay here anymore," he said.

Neva looked so small in her oversized winter coat, but she couldn't stop talking: "Look at this, Mom! They let me help! This is so cool!"

I led Jude back to the house while Neva stayed in the machine shop the rest of the day. At the time I wondered if I'd done the wrong thing. I worried that Neva was too excited by death or that Jude would be forever traumatized by what he'd witnessed. I'd grown up in a big city, so I had no parenting reference points for this. Maybe Jude's later fascination with death came out of that moment. Maybe Neva's excitement was in reaction to the trauma of her dog bite. Or maybe I was just reading into things.

Even though we were living in rural Illinois, my fears were particular to my urban upbringing. Children who grow up on farms or in rural communities that depend on farms for their lifeblood have traditionally had a totally different relationship to food and, as a result, to death.

Our culture is used to outsourcing many things related to death, and food is no exception. Fewer of us grow, raise, or kill the food we eat, so we can easily overlook death's role in the process. Before I lived on a farm or butchered chickens, I was a lifelong meat-eater, uncomfortable with a hunter's enthusiasm in killing food to feed their families. I had purchased countless boneless, skinless chicken breasts but couldn't imagine killing a bird with my own hands.

My ancestors, many of them from poor rural farms, were more used to dealing with death. They slaughtered and cooked the animals they raised from calves or chicks or piglets. Their children witnessed and participated in all aspects of food preparation.[1]

Without that kind of death, their survival was in jeopardy. In his book *The Slavery of Death*, psychology professor Dr. Richard Beck says there are different kinds of human anxieties in relation to death. Basic anxiety is "the anxiety of biological survival . . . our fight-or-flight response."[2] For my ancestors, death was often related to this basic anxiety of survival, whether they would have enough to eat, whether their crops would survive a bad storm and they would starve, whether their babies (or mothers) would die in childbirth. Farming parents of the past probably didn't worry the way I did that their kids were being introduced to death too early because death was woven into the fabric of their lives.

I don't understand what it means to fear for my life with such immediacy. Not only am I *not* afraid that I won't survive the day but my lack of proximity to death also gives me the false notion that I have a large measure of power over my eventual demise. In a culture like mine where I am so far from the painful realities of so many, fear of death expresses itself as neurotic anxiety.[3]

Neurotic anxiety is "characterized by worries, fears, and apprehensions associated with our self-concept . . . driven by how we compare ourselves to those in our social world."[4] We see this anxiety increasing with social media and the access we have to all the people in the world with which we can compare ourselves. We also see this neurotic anxiety when it comes to the ways we parent our children.

Living on a farm and being closer to death put my own parenting fears in sharper focus. While the desire to ensure my children's safety and well-being is, of course, natural and necessary, I wonder how my parenting might change if I paid more attention to the ways my fear of death and neurotic anxiety creep into our lives.

***

One of my sharpest memories from elementary school is of the blood dripping over my classmate's brow when he fell off the giant wooden dinosaur playscape that one of our teachers had built in the school playground. After a few stitches, my classmate was fine, and I'm sure he climbed right back on the dinosaur after he healed. But the dinosaur playscape didn't survive much longer.

The parks and playscapes of my childhood looked very different to many of the parks of today. When I was a child, we chased each other through pebbled playgrounds in the shadow of that dinosaur. We got dizzy from creaky merry-go-rounds that lurched and tipped as we held on to keep from flying out into the gravel. We hid in concrete tunnels away from the ears of adults, sharing the quiet excitement of secrets. We bobbed on rusty seesaws whose rapid rebounds left cuts and bruises on our chins. We climbed thin metal ladders to the tops of steep narrow slides as high as tree branches.

Things have changed since then. The parks that my children play in, if they were built in the last few decades, have specially cushioned ground cover that bounces when you walk. Merry-go-rounds have seats with curved backs so that no one slides out. Seesaws have been replaced with colorful balance beams just inches from the ground.

There are so many good reasons to rethink the construction of our old playgrounds, both for the safety of our children and so that children with disabilities or mobility issues can have a place to explore and play too. Oddly enough, though, even with all of these playground modifications, the statistics of childhood injury and death haven't changed much since the 1980s. And in fact, there is evidence that certain injuries are increasing as a direct result of these specially cushioned parks. According to Hanna Rosin in the *Atlantic*, this could be due to "risk compensation"—children aren't accustomed to needing to be careful on the harder surfaces of our childhood playgrounds so they get injured more frequently. David Ball, a professor of risk management, says that "we have come to think of accidents as preventable and not a natural part of life."[5]

I've struggled with fears about safeguarding my children. I once believed that if I tried hard enough, I could protect them from harm. But life has shown me the ugly truth. Each of my four children has been to the emergency room for some reason or another: one for a dog bite, one for asthma exacerbated by a virus, one for a clavicle that got fractured while doing somersaults *on a carpet* in the living room, and one for a massive splinter from climbing on top of the monkey bars. Accidents will happen, even if we are hypervigilant.

Part of the upsetting reality of parenting is that even if we can protect our children from every physical injury, other things can hurt them, things that life throws at them that we might not anticipate. Friends will hurt them, they will fail, and they will be injured. Sometimes, as much as we love them, they will even be hurt by us.

Protecting my children from trauma and harm is part of my task as a parent. But overprotecting them, even if it does keep them from physical harm, can actually lead to other problems. Anxiety and depression are on the rise. There are myriad reasons for this, but many psychologists are warning that parenting fears are leading to epidemic levels of anxiety in our children.[6] Children whose parents try to protect them from every danger suffer from a lack of confidence and the fear of being independent. When we take over management of their lives or stop them from trying out potentially dangerous things, they receive the message that they aren't capable of learning boundaries, of managing their environment, of learning independence. We aren't raising them to believe they are capable of being self-reliant, of facing the scary world when they are ready with our love and trust behind them.

Some parents and communities are noticing these anxiety epidemics. In Wales, a playground called the Land is structured for potentially dangerous play: though they are lightly supervised, children are given opportunities to make fires, create trampolines from used mattresses, cut and hammer old boards and discarded pieces of furniture, and swing on an old rope over a creek.[7] Though each of us parents might have different ways of giving our kids more freedom depending on where we live, I see good in encouraging independence for children whose culture tells them that perfect and perfectly safe lives are possible.

When we first moved away from our farm to a small town, one of the things we missed the most was that our kids wouldn't be able to explore the world in the same ways they had on our 180 acres. They wouldn't have a creek or a forest to discover, hay lofts to climb, chickens to chase and raise, wood to nail together, discarded metal parts to fashion into sculptures. Even an electric fence to get shocked on a time or two.

It was Matthew who insisted that our older children be encouraged to have some freedom in our small town. The first time we let Jude ride his bike to the park and sit under a tree by the pond for an hour, he returned looking peaceful, a confident quality to his voice as he explained what he'd observed about his surroundings. I could tell that this small independence would be a lifeline for him when his days of sitting still at school left him emotionally weary and needing a physical outlet. We were trying, in our imperfect way, to show our kids that we trusted them—even if I was afraid to do so. I was learning that discernment and wisdom, and not fear, could dictate the way we raised our kids.

Children are resilient, particularly when they have been given opportunities to thrive and learn and grow, to be afraid, to do things that might get them some scrapes, splinters, mild burns, and occasionally, a few broken bones. Still, many people don't have the choice to move to a different home or city, to find the perfect parks to play in. Some communities don't even have access to parks at all.

D. L. Mayfield, author of *The Myth of the American Dream*, has written extensively about what it looks like to live in communities that are underserved. She describes stepping up to the microphone at a town hall meeting in order to beg the city council not to "tear down our neighborhood's one and only park to build a 'revitalization' project complete with brew pubs and shared workspaces." She recalls the emotion in her voice and the tension in her body when she told the council: "We have a moral responsibility to consider those who don't have resources and how we can best serve them."[8]

I'm ashamed to admit that until I had friends who taught me better, I never considered that some communities struggle to keep their parks running. I never considered that communities might have to fight to keep their one park. I never considered that my own fears could affect children other than my own.

***

Our fears for our children's safety, which are often rooted in a "neurotic" fear of death, can also harm children who are truly vulnerable. It's odd, then, that in towns like mine across America, quaint and prosperous towns where everyone knows the name of the local policemen, people are still afraid. We are afraid to let our children go to the park alone. We are afraid to let them use the play equipment without our hands-on supervision. We are afraid they will be injured, kidnapped, or killed.

One woman in a local shop told me she was afraid that her teenage daughter might be sex trafficked. And why wouldn't she be afraid? Various social media posts make the rounds describing some version of an incident in which a woman and her children are followed around a store or out to their car. The posts usually conclude that the strange men, often "ethnic looking," are trying to abduct the children for the purposes of sex trafficking.

It's easy to be swept up in this fear. We want to protect our kids from harm, and harm seems to be all around us. The problem is not that the dangers don't exist but that our fears are often misdirected. According to the FBI, missing children reports are 40 percent lower than they were more than a decade ago. That's staggering given that the population has increased 30 percent since then. The likelihood of a child being abducted by a stranger is incredibly low.[9]

But that doesn't mean there aren't children at risk.

Children are abducted quite often in our country, but they are more likely to be taken by a parent or family member, someone who knows them. And the upsetting truth about sex trafficking is that the United States has staggering numbers of people trafficked for sex and labor every year. However, the web of trafficking doesn't start from a stranger abducting a child from an attentive mother or father. Most trafficking victims have been "manipulated by people they already knew."[10]

My friends Beth, Taylor, and Tim live and work with addicts in the largest city in Ohio. Their program originally started in order to find a way to help people recover from drug addiction. After years of living and working with vulnerable populations, they realized that 100 percent of the women they encountered had been trafficked. Now they are finding new ways to tailor their program to victims of trafficking.

Human trafficking overwhelmingly happens to vulnerable women or children from abusive or neglected homes, children who have been in foster care, addicts, homeless teenagers (many of them LGBTQ), vulnerable kids who have been neglected and groomed by people they know, people from marginalized populations, migrant workers, men and women brought to the United States from overseas with a promise of good work. A grassroots movement is working to bring attention to the epidemic of missing women from Native American populations, many of whom have likely been trafficked as well.[11]

When we live our lives in fear and we perpetuate ill-informed fears about things like sex trafficking, we funnel energy away from the real victims. Lara Powers, a professional who works in anti-trafficking, says that after seeing thousands of cases of sex trafficking, she's "never seen, read or heard about a real sex-trafficking situation in which a child was abducted by traffickers in broad daylight at a busy store under a mother's watchful eye. It's just not the way it works."[12]

Powers notes that sex trafficking happens in larger numbers than we realize and should be taken seriously. Part of taking the epidemic seriously is being well informed. If watchful parents have any reason to be worried for their children, they should look to their mobile devices and watch who their children are talking to online. "Sex traffickers are social-media savvy," according to a Michigan State Police lieutenant who has seen many victims of sex trafficking. The bulk of cases her department investigates are developing on messaging apps.[13]

Certainly, all these intense fears we have about our children's safety come from the real tragedies that we see splashed across the news. When a child is abducted, our worst fears emerge. The injuring of a child is really the worst thing most of us can imagine. But the truth is, abduction by a stranger or an injury from playground equipment, though unthinkably tragic, is not always representative of what is going on every day.

When we spend so much emotional energy protecting our kids from any potential harm, we don't see those kids we could help, kids caught up in the foster care system, kids who need mentoring. Our fear of death, emerging in our parenting fears, can make it worse for children who are already vulnerable. Like George MacDonald taught us, facing our fear of death—and the ways that fear affects us and all of the children around us—will take courage.

But our entire communities, and not just our own family units, will be better for it.

PART IV

FUNERAL PRACTICES, RACISM, AND CLIMATE CHANGE: MYSTICS IN AMERICA

14

THE COMMUNAL RITUALS OF DEATH

My house has doors built for death. Constructed in the 1850s in Ohio, the house has narrow stairways that appear in unexpected places (and are perfect for hide-and-seek) and steps that creak and bend from more than a century of foot traffic.

As you climb one set of stairs to the older side of the house, two different colors of circus-striped wallpaper cover the bedrooms in a strangely charming way. The previous owner restored the old wood of door frames, built beautiful hearths, and remodeled the kitchen. One half of the house is undoubtedly original, at least in its structure.

It wasn't long after we moved into this old house that I began to wonder about our front doors, of which there were three. The door by the driveway seemed the most logical choice for a front door, so we placed our garden statue of Saint Francis of Assisi there to welcome visitors. But the two other doors on either side of our L-shaped porch—each with three steps leading up to it—confused our visitors.

We started finding packages delivered to each porch door, and knocks rattled across the house so that I wasn't sure which of the three doors a visitor had decided to try.

"What a strange thing, to have three doors," I said to one guest who'd grown up in the area.

"Oh," he said, "they're built for wakes. You know, to keep the line of people moving, from one door to the other."[1]

This information shook me, and I wondered, What kind of grief and loss had occurred here in the 168 years since the foundations were laid? I could suddenly imagine the bodies of those who had lived in our house laid out in our dining room, bodies prepared and mourned for. The widow mourning her elderly husband who died from heart disease or the wife who died in her sleep. Or worse heartaches that were painful to even imagine as I watched my four children play hide-and-seek across the house.

Around the time my house was built, people often died at home rather than in hospitals, and their families cared for the bodies. Typically, the deceased was washed and groomed by the women of the household and clothed in a simple home-sewn garment or "winding sheet," a cloth that, when wrapped around a body, made the dead resemble a mummy.[2] Sometimes a woman would sew her own death shroud.

Burial clothes have differed throughout history depending on culture and religious customs. Early Christians reacted against the Roman custom of burying their dead in their finest clothes. They chose simple shrouds for burial garments, taking their wisdom from priest, mystic, and perpetual grump Saint Jerome, who knew the social leveling power of death even in the fourth century: "Why should the dead be clothed in sumptuous vestments? Cannot the rich rot away unless in the same gorgeous apparel that decorated them when alive?"[3]

Traditional wakes in the United States before the 1880s were simple affairs: the deceased was generally laid out in a wooden coffin in a family room that was kept cool, sometimes with a tub full of an ice block underneath the body.[4] During the wake, friends and family would file through the house, paying their respects to the dead and supporting the family.

There is a scene in the novel *The Shipping News* by Annie Proulx where a small fishing community is having a wake for Jack Buggit, a middle-aged man who drowned while fishing. In a climactic moment, while Jack is laid out in his family's home, he sits straight up on the table, leaving his mourners in temporary shock. It turns out that Mr. Buggit was not nearly as dead as they thought.

It's an unexpected moment of levity but also a good illustration of one of the practical reasons for wakes, at least for our ancestors who didn't have the luxury of coroners and morticians to confirm a person's death. Wakes were used for a variety of reasons. In earlier times, people were assigned to watch bodies so that animals, pests, and flies wouldn't overtake the corpse before it was time to be buried. But most especially, wakes ensured that the dead were truly dead.

As we know, fears about being buried alive plagued Victorians (the workhouse poor and the wealthy alike), but these fears also troubled ancient peoples. The ancient Celts, Jews, and Romans waited days before burial to make sure the body began to decay. Romans would also shout the person's name and cut off a finger to see if it bled before burning the dead on a funeral pyre. In the New Testament, Jesus surprises Mary Magdalene by being alive while she was following the Jewish custom of returning every day for three days to watch for his body.[5]

Even though wakes aren't typical anymore in our Western culture, we probably think of them as sober times for grief. But some cultures have chosen to use wakes not just for mourning but for celebrations. The Scottish held what they called a "lykewake" in which mourners who wanted to avoid dreaming of the dead touched the deceased with their left hands. The party, fueled by alcohol, tobacco, and feasting, started later. Fake duels were staged. A person acting in the role of the deceased would pretend to be killed and resurrected by a stand-in for a sorcerer. Of course, not everyone was partying: those designated as "weeping women" would continue to mourn the dead in the corner.[6]

Some traditional cultures held wakes so that their loved ones' bodies could decompose naturally. Whereas wakes could last a few days to a week in some places, in the indigenous tribes of Indonesia and the Philippines wakes could last for months or years. This protracted wake allowed the deceased to mummify or decompose naturally until the burial time was set.[7]

The tradition of wakes also had purposes in the spiritual and emotional life of the community. Many of the mourning rituals began at the wake, giving permission to both the individual mourner and the community to grieve as a necessity. With the removal of death from our homes and communal spaces, we have lost something significant. I'm not sure we always know how to leave space for grief anymore.

***

I was a mother of two when my grandfather Papa died in his nineties. Long gone were the days of drinking Diet Dr Pepper and white wine with his wife, Oneta, while Papa looked on in mild disapproval. When he died, we were already living in Illinois on a farm. Papa could never quite understand why we would choose farm life. His father had been a poor tenant farmer, moving his seven children around desolate farms in West Texas during the Great Depression, never making enough. For Papa, farm life represented hardship. And he wasn't far off the mark.

Papa was a storyteller. Our childhood was full of his tales about what life was like for a boy from a poor farm family: clothes with holes in them, sharing a bed with several of his six siblings, being mocked relentlessly by his older sisters when he wet the bed, eating cereal with water because they couldn't afford milk. The most tragic of all was the day his mother accidentally left a fistful of cash in their car when it broke down. When she returned, it was all gone. She left the family not long after and moved to the city.

My grandfather left home at the age of fourteen, already the shape and size of a man. He lied about his age so he could get work. He hopped trains, had part of his finger severed while changing a tire on an old Ford, became a firefighter, and eventually enlisted in World War II. His ship was captured before he ever saw battle, and so he spent three years as a prisoner of war in Japan.

Papa was a military man, and he and my grandmother moved thirty-four times during their marriage. My sisters and I knew him as a jolly grandfather who played with us, laughed with us, made breakfast for us, and adored us. With his white beard and hair and rotund belly, he was often tapped to play Santa Claus at various Christmas functions. Even off-season, children would stop him in restaurants and think he was Santa. He loved the attention and had a booming laugh and an extraverted personality to fit the part.

He looked very different at the funeral home, his body laid in an open coffin just before the visitation. Designed for ease and comfort, the funeral home had overstuffed comfy chairs, soft music playing, and low, measured murmurs as mourners drifted in and out. It was only just a tad like a home, as if aliens had taken notes on what a human home looked like but left out specific homish elements. I'm not saying that funeral home directors are aliens; but the service they offer (often for thousands of dollars) is something that used to be done in an *actual* home. There is something not quite right about a place attempting to be something that it is not.

Jessica Mitford's 1963 book *The American Way of Death* (updated in the '90s to reflect some, but not enough, industry changes) gives a scathing account of the unethical practices of the funeral industry. The funeral industry of Mitford's day had made burial into a business of unnecessary expenditure: extra-comfort caskets, embalming practices that cause seepage of hundreds of gallons of harmful chemicals into the earth, and savvy industry folks who could, if they wanted, take advantage of the confusion and disorientation brought on by grief.

Mitford famously said that the funeral industry had played "a huge, macabre, and expensive practical joke on the American public."[8]

It's not that clear that things have changed much since Mitford wrote her book. Funeral costs in the United States have been rising for decades, particularly for those wanting a full-service funeral from a funeral home. A funeral home typically charges a nondeclinable basic fee of $2,000, and from there a list of other fees include body transportation, body preparation, embalming, a hearse, a casket, facilities, and staff for the viewing and the service. These conventional funerals can cost $6,000–$8,000, a range that doesn't include the price of gravestones or funeral plots, which can also total in the thousands. When it comes to grieving families, funeral industries are in the prime position to take advantage of mental and emotional stress.[9]

The cost of a casket alone can set a family back thousands of dollars. When my friend Steve lost his father to cancer, he was flabbergasted by the coffin choices he was shown at the funeral home. He describes one coffin as a '50s-model Cadillac of caskets, sleek and shiny and totally ugly. It would cost upwards of $3,000 to be seen for just two days.

Steve refused to pay so much, and instead he and his family came up with a solution. He remembered the funeral of a friend from the year before who had been buried in a simple homemade casket. Why couldn't they do that instead? They found the same guy who'd made his friend's coffin and bought the last one off of him. The simple, beautiful, handmade coffin cost $400. Years later, Steve decided he'd save his family from the grief of having to find him a coffin. He also wanted to take some time to face his own death, whenever that might occur. So he made his own. It's sitting on a shelf in his woodshop.

My grandfather didn't have the Cadillac of coffins, but it was sleek and polished, lying open in the plush visitation room of the funeral home. His terminal illness had thinned him and sapped his vigor, but still, he looked so unlike our Santa Claus. His body had been embalmed, and his skin was pallid, waxlike. His smile looked off, too tight at the corners, as if someone had placed their palms on his cheeks and pulled them away from each other.

In *Grave Matters*, a book about everything from green burial alternatives to the modern funeral, Mark Harris spends an entire chapter describing methods of modern embalming. It's a gruesome read, and I had to take breaks when I read it. He details the invasive surgical practices used by funeral directors to make a person's body presentable to their living loved ones.

The rather shortened (and sanitized) version is that all of the blood in the entire body is drained and replaced with embalming fluids, like formaldehyde and dyes that brighten and preserve the skin. The mouth is sewn, glued, or clamped shut so as not to disturb mourners, the eyelids glued together, and many of the contents of the body cavity are sucked out through a tube inserted into the abdomen. "Embalming restores a lifelike appearance to the deceased," Harris says. "Refrigeration does not, which may only matter if you expect the dead to resemble the living."[10]

Death obviously brings changes to a body over time, but the irony is that my grandfather, even embalmed, didn't look like his former self. He looked different in an unnatural way, like a pillow that's been washed and then dried lumpy. How our culture has changed its traditions of burial and has come to expect the dead to look like the living is a long, sometimes disturbing, and fascinating history.

***

Embalming has been around for a really long time. Some cultures arrived at their own forms of embalming, from preserving the body in honey to enclosing the body in wax. The Egyptians were most well known for the practice—done for religious reasons—that began around 3200 BCE. Though they differed in practice, there is evidence from 600 CE that the Paracas of Peru embalmed their dead as well as the Incans and some early Native tribes of America.[11]

Before the Civil War, American Christians were in line with the religious beliefs of Jews, Muslims, and Baha'i who all rejected embalming because of its connections with ancient Egyptian or pagan rituals. They believed that such practices defaced the body, a body that, for Christians, was considered a temple of the Holy Spirit.[12] Buddhists and Hindus didn't need embalming as they preferred cremation.[13]

But during the Civil War many families began turning to the ancient practice of embalming, all thanks to an industrious man who had an enthusiasm for dissection and cadavers. In the beginning of the Civil War, a soldier's regiment might have taken charge of returning his body from the battlefield to his home many miles away, but gradually, families began sending loved ones to fetch the remains. In those hot crowded trains, as people returned home, bodies decomposed rapidly, and the smell became difficult to bear.

Enter onto the scene the enterprising Thomas H. Holmes. It might give us a glimpse into the personality of Holmes to know that he used the title "Dr." all of his life even though he'd been kicked out of medical school. Holmes was brought to fame in 1861 when his great masterpiece was displayed in the White House and New York. His magnum opus was the embalmed body of the war hero Colonel Ellsworth, displayed in an open casket.

Holmes's work must have been a success because the army, thereafter, commissioned him to embalm bodies during wartime. Most of his money in embalming came not from the army but from private hiring, and other embalmers took advantage of the business opportunity of wartime embalming. Sometimes embalmers, looking to make a fast dollar, even fought over bodies on the battlefield. It got so bad that the War Department had to issue an order that only licensed embalmers could work with families to take care of their dead in war.[14]

Embalming solutions during the Civil War were dangerous for the health of the living. Though many of the chemicals used in modern embalming are still carcinogens, the embalming solutions of the past were even worse. Practitioners often died from the repeated use of chemicals like mercury and arsenic in embalming. But the practices of embalming enabled families to bury loved ones who had died on the battlefield in the family plot. When President Lincoln died and his body was embalmed in order to preserve it for a viewing tour around the country, the practice became acceptable in wider, polite society.[15]

Holmes came home from the war in good shape. Claiming to have embalmed at least four thousand soldiers in four years of the war, he was a rich man.[16] However, his final years were not so happy. It is said that Holmes actually spent his last years in mental institutions. Some wonder if the effects of his work, and the chemicals used during embalming, caused Holmes to go insane.[17]

After the Holmes era of embalming, formaldehyde replaced arsenic as the main ingredient in embalming solutions, and the funeral industry flourished. Embalming chemicals were patented and funeral directors given expert status. Families, many of whom had once been active participants in the tactile, tangible acts of body preparation, were relegated to the position of observers at a museum of waxen corpses; hands that were once engaged in the physical parts of grief were now empty and restless, and people wandered through a funeral business made to look like a home.

I wonder what kind of experience it would've been if my Papa's body had been cared for by his loved ones. The practice hasn't been passed down through the generations, so the social acceptability of such a way of burial has diminished.

But many today are eschewing this kind of passive burial for a ceremony that resembles those held by my ancestors. Proponents of a return to the traditional way of burial practiced before the Civil War claim that preparing a loved one's body can be a beautiful and healing experience, even if, God forbid, the loved one is a child.

For Beth, a woman who had to face the unimaginable death of her child, caring for her six-year-old daughter's body helped her accept the reality of her daughter's death. Afterward, Beth became a "death-care midwife," teaching people across the country how to prepare their loved ones' bodies for burial. Beth believes that with the right preparation, the natural condition of the body after a three-day wake helps the bereaved let go of the loved one: "The body is often beautiful that first day . . . by the third day, the deceased begins to look like an empty shell, and it's often at that point that a family may be ready to let go."[18]

While embalming might attempt to make a body appear closer to what the person looked like before death, Beth's experience suggests that perhaps this appearance isn't as therapeutic as allowing the decaying body to guide a mourner into a natural process of grief. Perhaps the act of caring for the deceased's physical body can help us mourn in another way.

While funeral homes serve a purpose that is often necessary in our society, in the past, it was the women and men of your community who would surround you, not only with food but also with their physical help in preparing the body, in building the coffin, in digging the grave, in planning a service. As strange as some of them might seem to us, most of these traditions have that in common: these death rituals were carried out in community. A people with a history, with family, with communal memories and rituals, find ways to grieve together and manage the reality of death. In our modern culture, where community is often fractured, many people have become disconnected from the shared death rituals of the past.

Even in the 1940s when mystic Howard Thurman gave his Ingersoll lecture at Harvard, death practices in the United States had changed greatly. Thurman said that as death moved out of the home and into the hospital and the mortuary, "our primary relationship with death [became] impersonal and detached."[19]

Thurman's astute observations are still relevant many years later. Perhaps even more so. When we are so far removed from death, the result is a strain on our emotional lives. According to Thurman, "tremendous emotional blocks are set up without release, making for devious forms of inner chaos, which cause us to limp through the years with our griefs unassuaged."[20] The people who perform our funeral rituals are doing us a service, to be sure, but often our relationship with them is purely transactional rather than communal. We've forgotten the communal rituals that used to help us experience death. And with those losses, our cultural relationship with death is actually dangerous to our emotional health.

15

THE TENSIONS OF DEATH AND LIFE

Enlightenment thinkers celebrated the progress and exploration they brought to the rest of the world. But even as they cheered these advancements, the thinkers and explorers were turning a blind eye to (or actively participating in) unthinkable atrocities: millions of Africans were kidnapped from their homes to fuel the slave trade; colonists heaped war, death, and disease upon the indigenous peoples of America. By 1750, all thirteen original colonies of the United States had enslaved people. By 1770, black enslaved people made up 21 percent of the population of the Americas.[1]

By the beginning of the nineteenth century, ten to fifteen million people from Africa had been transported as slaves to the Americas to be sold and bought. All told, it is estimated that "Africa lost 50 million human beings to death and slavery in those centuries we call the beginnings of modern Western civilization, at the hands of slave traders and plantation owners in Western Europe and America, the countries deemed the most advanced in the world."[2]

How could the Enlightenment and these atrocities exist in such contrast?

Although racialized prejudice has a long and ancient history, it was actually *because of* Enlightenment advances in scientific thought that an "enduring racial taxonomy and the 'color-coded, white-over-black' ideology" was created, according to journalist Jamelle Bouie. Indeed, Bouie sees "race as we understand it—a biological taxonomy that turns physical difference into relations of domination—[as] a product of the Enlightenment."[3]

William Blake, a mystical poet born in 1757 in England, has often been hailed as a visionary whose poetic words and insightful illustrations were progressive by the standards of his age. Much has been written of his poetry and the fact that Blake was fervently antislavery. One scholar in 1952 called Blake's book *Visions of the Daughters of Albion* an "abolitionist parable."[4] But scholar David Bindman takes a closer look. William Blake was entrenched in certain views of whiteness and blackness, views that emerge even in his abolitionist writing.

Blake's poem "The Little Black Boy," which was likely intended to show compassion for the plight and suffering of enslaved people, uses language that gives us a picture of "blackness" and "whiteness" during the Enlightenment. In it, Blake writes from the perspective of a suffering child:

> My mother bore me in the southern wild,
> And I am black, but O! my soul is white;
> White as an angel is the English child:
> But I am black as if bereav'd of light.[5]

Blake uses the word *black* as an undesirable state of being, a state that needs redeeming in eternity. Even as the boy in the poem is suffering because of the color of his skin, his desire, according to Blake, is always for spiritual purity. The color of this purity, of his soul, is white. And blackness is a state that must be escaped.

Though he professed disgust with slavery, Blake still wasn't free from the false and dangerous notions passed down from the Enlightenment, notions that placed African blackness as inherently subservient to European whiteness. Bindman says that Blake was, like many in his time, entrenched in "the complex and often contradictory web of ancient and modern beliefs that had settled around Africa and Africans in the late eighteenth century."[6]

Blake wasn't alone in being embedded in a biased belief system that, despite his professed views, led to his complicity in the oppression of others. Sometimes our worldviews and biases are so intricately bound up in cultural understandings that untangling them takes work, energy, and humility. Facing our fear of death can be just as complicated because it also means that we might have to uncover our own bigotries.

Though slavery has been abolished and legal segregation is a thing of the past, in the grand narrative of Western civilization, it hasn't been that long since bigotry was legal. What began more than four hundred years ago, when the first enslaved people were stolen from Africa, has only been illegal in the United States since the 1950s when segregation was abolished. That encompasses the bulk of our history.

Racism continues to leak into our social and political

systems. And because we are entrenched in our own cultural and belief systems, we don't always see it.

***

As the first occupants began to make a home among the hearth fires of my Ohio house in 1851, a few hours away in Akron, a black woman rose from the audience of a crowded church and made her way to the front. She loomed large over them, standing at six feet tall, wearing wire-rimmed glasses, her head covered in a bonnet.[7]

Some in the audience had tried stop her from speaking that day, worried that the distraction of her skin color would label them as agitators, ruining their cause for women's rights.

But Sojourner Truth was on a mission of liberation, and she wouldn't be swayed or intimidated. She had fought for the abolition of enslaved people, but she also saw that her fight was necessary for women of all colors. She stepped onto the stage at the Women's Rights Convention in Akron and began to speak.

Sojourner Truth was named Isabella in 1797 by her enslavers on a large plantation in New York state. Like all of the other enslaved people of the estate, including her parents and siblings, she was forced to sleep in the cellar, something she shuddered to recall later in her autobiography. She describes its occupants as "inmates, of both sexes and all ages, sleeping on those damp boards, like the horse, with a little straw and a blanket." She remembers the pain endured by those sleeping arrangements, "the rheumatisms, and fever-sores, and palsies, that distorted the limbs and racked the bodies of those fellow-slaves."[8]

Truth's childhood was ravaged by traumas. In her earliest years, her loving mother and father, both of them enslaved, would tell her stories of her older siblings, sisters and brothers Truth never knew because they had been taken from their parents and sold. Truth had a brother who was just a little boy when "on the last morning he was with them, [he] arose with the birds, kindled a fire, calling for his Mau-mau to 'come, for all was now ready for her'—little dreaming of the dreadful separation which was so near at hand."[9] As a young girl Truth would often find her mother crying, reliving a separation from one of her children that would "crucify her heart afresh."[10] Her parents' "hearts still bled," for each of their lost children.[11]

Even in the midst of her pain, Truth's mother would tell her about a God who saw their every heartache, a God who knew their every pain, a God to whom they should cry out in prayer. Pray to God, her mother said, "when you are beaten, or cruelly treated, or fall into any trouble, you must ask help of him, and he will always hear and help you." Then Truth's mother would groan, crying out in the psalmist's words, "Oh Lord, how long?"[12]

Truth took her mother's advice to heart. Even as a child, she found profound comfort in God. She escaped daily to "a small island in a small stream, covered with large willow shrubbery, beneath which the sheep had made their pleasant winding paths." She arranged tree branches so that they formed an outdoor church for her, "a circular arched alcove, made entirely of the graceful willow." In this makeshift church, away from her enslavers and onlookers, she could commune with God, speaking aloud in the safety of her shelter.[13]

When Truth was just nine years old, she says, "her trials in life" began. She was sent to the auction block and sold for a hundred dollars, separating her from her parents. Her new enslavers couldn't understand Truth's first language, Dutch, and for those misunderstandings, they whipped her with cords heated in the fire until her "flesh was deeply lacerated, and the blood streamed from her wounds."[14]

When she was sold again to the Dumont family, her trials and abuse were so bad that she refrained from detailing many of the specifics in her autobiography.

Truth was forced into marriage with another enslaved man named Thomas who had already been forcibly separated from his first two wives. Truth recalls that their ceremony was a "mock marriage" because "no true minister of Christ can perform, as in the presence of God, what he knows to be a mere farce . . . unrecognised by any civil law, and liable to be annulled any moment, when the interest or caprice of the master should dictate."[15]

When Truth eventually gave birth to five children, she lamented that she had been forced to birth "on the altar of slavery—a sacrifice to the bloody Moloch."[16] One of her sons was sold as a five-year-old and illegally taken South, and though she searched for him and pleaded with the people who sold him, it took Truth three years to be reunited with him.

How could Sojourner Truth bear such atrocities? How was she able to bear the separation from her family and her community? In *Knowing Christ Crucified: The Witness of African American Religious Experience*, professor of theology M. Shawn Copeland says one emancipated woman shared that Jesus was the reason she was able to live in the midst of such violence. "He's held me up," the woman said. "I'd' er died long ago without him."[17] Copeland says that many enslaved people knew Jesus as someone who suffered with them. The faith of enslaved peoples in the crucified Lord was "no act of self-abnegation" but instead "an act of signifying resistance."[18] They had the comfort of a God who, like Truth's mother taught, saw them, and loved them.

Truth turned to God often in her life, and when she needed wisdom to help her gain freedom, she heard God's voice. In 1827, slavery was officially ended in New York, allowing Truth her freedom. But her enslavers refused.

Truth consulted God for discernment. She told God that "she was afraid to go in the night, and in the day every body would see her." A thought then came to her directly from God that she could make her escape just before daybreak. She obeyed: just before dawn, she took her infant and walked away from the Dumonts.[19]

Her walk to freedom wasn't over, though. Mr. Dumont found her and demanded that she return to him. It was the moment that she began to follow that Truth had a mystical experience. Truth explains that "God revealed himself to her, with all the suddenness of a flash of lightning, showing her, 'in the twinkling of an eye, that he was *all over*'—that he pervaded the universe—'and that there was no place where God was not.'" When she came back to herself, Dumont had left.[20]

She eventually took the name Sojourner Truth when God whispered it to her; it was a name that would describe her travels as she fought for freedom for many years, speaking only "truth" to all people.

When Sojourner finally stepped up to the stage in Akron in 1851 many years later, she was part of the movement to encourage Ohio lawmakers to make sure that their new constitution expanded the legal rights of women.[21] It had been a decade since abolitionists Lucretia Mott and Elizabeth Cady Stanton had been barred from attending the World Anti-Slavery Convention in London because they were women. Their exclusion only energized their activism, and the Women's Rights Convention, held annually in the United States, was born.

It would still be nearly fifty years before white women would be allowed to vote. Though black women—who had worked untiringly for the rights of *all* women for many decades—finally got the right to vote in 1920, it wasn't until the Voting Rights Act of 1965 that racial discrimination in voting practices was banned.

Some of the women present at the convention in 1851 would co-opt Truth's speech for their own agendas and largely ignore her and other black suffragists in their *History of Woman Suffrage.* Still, on that stage in Akron, Sojourner Truth, a woman who was formerly enslaved, stood up to speak for the rights of all women.

Her speech is famously known as the "Ain't I a Woman" speech. But Sojourner Truth never spoke those words in her speech. Feminist Frances Gage later published an inaccurate version of Truth's speech, giving Truth a Southern "mammy caricature" dialect.[22] But Truth was not Southern. Her first language was Dutch, and though she learned and spoke English, she never lost her accent.

Gage's changes, though they inspired many, were made to appeal to white women.

You can go to the Sojourner Truth Project's website and listen to versions of Truth's speech, read by women of Afro-Dutch descent, that more fully embody Truth's heritage, inflection, humor, and strength.[23] Speaking to the Ohio legislature and to all men, she said, "I have as much muscle as any man, and can do as much work as any man," and "I can carry as much as any man, and can eat as much too, if I can get it."[24] Unlike Gage's version, Truth spoke to the intellect of woman. She spoke to the "poor" confused men of the nation, calling them "children" and telling them that they would feel better if they just gave women their rights: "You need not be afraid to give us our rights for fear we will take too much," she said. "You will have your own rights, and they won't be so much trouble."[25]

Sojourner Truth got to see abolition come to fruition in her life, but even after the Emancipation Proclamation of 1863, she still worked tirelessly for women's suffrage and the rights of the emancipated. She saw the end of the Civil War and visited President Lincoln. She died of old age among her family in Battle Creek, Michigan.

***

Sojourner Truth experienced unimaginable horrors in her life. Like Truth, enslaved people lived in the tension of "death-in-life" caused by the trauma and terror of slave ships and the plantation systems of chattel slavery, where people were treated as personal property to be bought and sold.[26] Howard Thurman used haunting imagery to imagine the injustice and violence that his own ancestors experienced on slave ships. Death "at the hand of nature" disturbs us to the core, he wrote, "but death at the hands of another human being makes for panic in the mind and outrages the spirit. . . . The human spirit is stripped to the literal substance of itself."[27]

What wisdom did enslaved people have from their trauma, their knowledge of all of the horrors that those who fear death can bring? Copeland says that the "wisdom of the enslaved people" was "apophatic or dark wisdom," a kind of wisdom that is "expressed in paradox, a wisdom that countered the wisdom of the world."[28]

In the mystic tradition, there are various ways of speaking of God. In the more familiar *kataphatic* or positive way, the mystics speak of seeking God by contemplating God's perfection: God is loving, kind, and just, a good and wise creator who offers relationship to all of creation.

But in the mystical tradition, there is also the apophatic way, *via negativa*. The usage of the *negativa* doesn't mean that mystics are speaking ill of God. Instead, the negative way is paradoxical and therefore more puzzling: it says that we know God by knowing that we cannot know God. God is so wholly *other* that any metaphor we use to describe God will fall short, so it shouldn't be attempted.[29]

Mystics like Saint John of the Cross, Meister Eckhart, and fourteenth-century German mystic Johannes Tauler approached God with this paradox. It's not that they thought God unknowable. Instead, they extolled "knowing God by way of unknowing, that is, by the failing of knowledge."[30] A Dominican priest who provided spiritual direction to nuns, Tauler's work was more accessible than some of the other apophatic-leaning mystics. He had a "strong affirmative spirituality" that balanced out this *via negativa*, and he believed in the great power of love.[31] Tauler believed that the way to union with God was through "self-dying," a spiritual process of letting God's will overcome his own.[32]

There is complexity and paradox and mystery in seeking God. Though there are biblical passages that could be used to express both kataphatic and apophatic ways of seeking, the paradox is that God is both hidden and unknowable *and* God is incarnate, fleshly, and intimate with us. We see all of these attributes in Jesus.

Because of Jesus's incarnation and suffering on the cross, enslaved people like Sojourner Truth knew that Jesus understood the "dark and hidden wisdom": the knowledge of the way of death. The cross of Christ rejected the "death dealing" of the enslaver, whose very way of being in the world was death and violence.[33] The power of resurrection was that "death would not be the last word, that slavery would not be the last word. The God who vindicated Jesus would vindicate them."[34]

Howard Thurman talks of the consolation of black spirituals, songs, and hymns, often written by enslaved people in the midst of death and violence. Sometimes these spirituals were also "codified protest songs" that served as a "secret language" for enslaved people to seek freedom.[35]

"Oh Freedom! Oh Freedom!" chants one such spiritual.[36] "I want to die easy when I die," sings another.[37] In such lyrics we hear that in the climate of chattel slavery, death wasn't "life's worst offering," according to Thurman. Spirituals offered a picture of death as liberation and promised that "death itself . . . is not the master of life," often brutal but never "triumphant."[38]

These hopeful spirituals were an "affirmation ringing in their ears" that enslaved people could "stand anything that life could bring against them."[39] Spirituals expressed enslaved people's belief that God was their champion and knew them intimately.[40] Many escaped to sanctuaries like the one Sojourner Truth created with her willow branches, in order to "experience God in their misery and obscurity."[41] Thurman speaks of the *kataphatic* way of knowing: the "secret" of enslaved people's courage and "ascendency over circumstances and the basis of their assurances concerning life and death" was that God was a "personal, intimate, and active" God who knew what it was to suffer and therefore was close to those who were also suffering.[42]

***

Spirituals, in general, don't mention the "slave owner." Thurman says that this absence of the slave owner or enslaver from these songs was evidence that enslavers were considered to be "outside the pale of moral and ethical responsibilities."[43] In other words, all that was expected from the enslaver was "gross evil."[44] This is chilling, especially for those of us whose ancestors might've been involved in such evil.

I don't know if any of my ancestors were enslavers. Still, I remember hearing a racist trope in one particular childhood story. My grandmother told us that somewhere in our past, we were related to the brother of the Confederate general Robert E. Lee. I don't know if this is true or not because it has been said that most southerners believe they are related to the general, but I do know that this was offered not as a shameful bit of family history, but as a fun family fact. In a school project "about me" from third grade, I wrote that I was related to Lee, as if he were a celebrity. There was certainly a familial acknowledgment that Lee had fought for the "wrong side," but that was excused in the next breath: he was fighting with his family members and for his beloved state of Virginia . . . family was more important than conscience.

Of course, that was assuming Lee *had* a conscience against slavery. It took me a number of years to realize that this bit of excusing was common in the "myth of Lee," invented to "erase slavery as the cause of the war and whitewash the Confederate cause as a noble one." The truth is that Lee fought to preserve slavery and was an enslaver himself. He punished his runaway slaves with beatings.[45]

If our country had listened to Frederick Douglass, the nineteenth-century abolitionist who was formerly enslaved, who spoke up after Lee's death, we might have avoided more than a century of propaganda. Douglass wrote scathingly of Lee in 1870, "'We can scarcely take up a newspaper . . . that is not filled with *nauseating* flatteries' of Lee, from which 'it would seem . . . that the soldier who kills the most men in battle, even in a bad cause, is the greatest Christian, and entitled to the highest place in heaven.'"[46]

I'm still learning about the myths perpetuated by my own worldview. Spiritual practitioner Talibah Chiku has seen that our fear of death shows up in many aspects of our lives. She says that "racism, violence, trauma, human destruction, and hate are all endemic in local, national, and worldwide atrocities, and epitomize the reality of attempting to delay one's mortality."[47] Racism continues to cut into the heart of our cultural fear of death, if only we have eyes to see it.

16

BETWEEN BIRTH AND DEATH

When I was pregnant with my fourth child, I could feel the difference in my thirty-nine-year-old body from when I'd had my first baby nearly a decade earlier. Within the first few weeks of pregnancy, it was as if my womb clocked the change, stood at attention, and said, "Yep, I remember this. Let's go for it!" My belly skipped straight to week eighteen and kept growing.

Compared to many, my body took to pregnancy relatively well, but in the last trimester, moving, sitting, sleeping, and even breathing became very difficult. A cough and cold in the weeks leading up to the birth got so bad that I had to sleep for days in a La-Z-Boy downstairs. I got bronchitis and had trouble climbing the stairs. The baby grew so active and heavy on my sore and aching joints that it felt like my uterus was no longer an adequate barrier between my baby and the world; one more painful, rib-cracking cough would shoot him out like Dumbo through a circus cannon.

Hip pain that began with my third pregnancy plagued me again in earnest. I was in so much discomfort that my midwife sent me to a chiropractor. I went into labor that night.

When you've been to the hospital enough times for birth, it becomes a familiar place. Every pregnant woman has her own stories of discomfort and pain. The history and theological understandings of pain in childbirth are fascinating, disturbing, and, at times, laughably naive. As Rachel Marie Stone notes in her book *Birthing Hope*, early male theologians declared that, because childbirth pains were viewed as Eve's curse in Genesis, any attempts to offer pain management to women was "an affront to God's wishes"; this pain supposedly taught women "temperance" and "reason."[1]

On the other hand, therapist Helen Wessel wrote a book in the 1970s for evangelical readers arguing that pain in childbirth wasn't actually biblical or inevitable. Wessel suggested that any pain a woman felt was merely her own "psychological or physical tension—not the physiological process of birth itself"[2] In either case, it seems that women cannot escape being blamed for their pain.

Like many women, I chose to give birth without pain medication but was reticent to talk about what these births truly meant to me, in an effort to avoid offending those who had different experiences. It became a sort of quiet truth I shared with few friends. With my first birth when I was thirty, I was swept up in this notion of Wessel's that birth could be both natural and pain-free: that with self-hypnosis, I, too, could avoid the pain of birth. During my actual labor, the pain caught me off guard, and I couldn't get a handle on it. When it was time for the baby to emerge and my midwife told me to bear down, all that classwork had failed to train me to push the baby out. Childbirth, regardless of how a baby is born, is often painful, and life just hurts sometimes too.

Almost three years after the birth of my fourth baby, my body can still feel carved out, slightly and permanently broken from giving life to others. Sometimes I feel like having children or giving birth was like Jacob wrestling with God. I got four babies as a blessing and the hip pain is the resulting wound. Although when I read that story, I find I don't feel all that sorry for Jacob and the wound he bore.

Let's be honest: he wasn't the best brother, husband, or father. He openly favored one wife and her sons over all the other children and mothers. Maybe when Jacob asked for a blessing and he received a crooked hip, God just wanted Jacob to have a tiny glimpse of what his wives and concubines went through to birth all those babies for his benefit. We get a small glimpse into the pains *they* bore with Leah's great suffering. But her pains in childbirth—perhaps they were just too commonplace to mention.

Because death has been a lifelong fixation for me, my decision to feel the birth pains felt like a battle against pain and death, a war against my view of my own weakness. I wondered: Could I truly do this hard thing? After my labors, birth and death became so connected in my mind that I often wondered if death would feel like childbirth.

***

In his first year of pastoring, Matthew was invited to the hospital to visit a congregant's elderly mother who was dying. The family of the mother was in the room, her children at her bedside, whispering words of love, holding her hand. Matthew had the overwhelming sense that her children were acting the way my midwife acted in my labors. They were midwifing her into death. This way of ushering the person into the next phase, of whispering words of affirmation and love, was very much like my husband's and my mother's role in my labors. During an ideal hospital death (if there is an ideal), as with a birth, the room is often full of loved ones, of expectation, of the tension of a coming release. As the elderly woman began to die, she was covered in prayer and love.

Often, the moment in birth when it feels impossible, when some birthing women say, "I can't do this anymore," is the time of transition. I had that moment in each of my births. The pain felt like it would undo me, like it was peeling all of my organs away from their connections inside me and dragging them out. I felt afraid during those first few births, like the pain would absolutely overpower me, and I would lose control. Once that juncture passed, birth began to move quickly. The baby's coming was imminent. The movement of something new was about to begin.

Maybe the same can be said of death. Death and birth are intricately entwined, even within our bodies. Dying is not a moment but a process, one that begins in the womb. Theologian Bethany Sollereder says that "from a biological point of view, death is . . . intrinsic, it's necessary to life."[3] She goes on to describe a normal biological process called apoptosis, by which our cells must die off to make room for new ones. Apoptosis, also called "programmed cell death," gets rid of cells that aren't functioning properly. When our cells are prevented from this process, when they begin multiplying instead of dying, we call that cancer.[4]

Apoptosis has the same prefix as *apophatic*—the *via negativa* way of approaching union with God. *Apo* means "away from" or "fall off." So both words are about a direction and a paradox. With the apophatic way, we know God more by admitting that God is unknowable. In apoptosis, parts of us must constantly die to make room for more life.

Death and life are wrapped up in this paradox, this constant pushing away and pulling toward. In this lifelong growing toward death, there is also a time of transition, an expansion to make room for that new phase to begin. Maybe this transition begins the moment we say, "I can't do this anymore." This is the time to pass through fear, knowing that the hardest part is coming but that you can and must get through it.

Like giving birth, this journey toward death is both solitary and communal. No one can give birth for you once the birthing has begun, and no earthly person can die for you either. Still, if we could die close to our community, maybe we wouldn't be so afraid. Maybe midwifing for one another in death makes us all feel less alone.

***

For many women, death and birth have been closer than just a philosophical connection. When our old house in Ohio was built, women often had their babies at home and had to face the fact that they could die in childbirth like many of their family members and neighbors had done.

Birth is a precarious place where the line between life and death is as thin as the membrane that holds a baby inside the womb. In my own company of women, we hold together miscarriages and stillbirths, dangerous maternal illnesses and conditions like preeclampsia, gestational diabetes, blood clots, and hyperemesis.

Stone's book describes the traumatic circumstances of birth in a Malawi hospital—as they labor with the worst maternal care in the world—where she observed women during her training to be a doula. It's a tragic picture.

But birth isn't only difficult for women in other countries. The horrible truth is that, while birth doesn't seem as dangerous as it used to for my ancestors who lived on remote farms in West Texas, women in the United States have shockingly high mortality rates. In fact, among Global North countries, the United States has the worst maternal death rate.[4]

And maternal death rates for black women are much worse: two to six times higher than that of white women.[5] This is a staggering statistic that should break all of us to pieces. It disturbed an obstetrician-gynecologist so much that he was forced to rethink his own biases in the way he offered healthcare. He realized that "when black women expressed concern about their symptoms, clinicians were more delayed and seemed to believe them less."[6]

For some women, these horrifying statistics might have something to do with the worries of economic hardship and access to healthcare, but black women also face an incredible amount of stress because of racism. Serena

Williams, one of the greatest tennis players of all time and a woman we might assume would have the best healthcare because she is famous and wealthy, had a life-threatening experience in the days after giving birth. Among other complications, despite her history of blood clots, her healthcare providers "did not act on her concern that she was experiencing a pulmonary embolism."[7] Williams eventually recovered, but her experience is not isolated.

Research in the 1990s and early 2000s connected the stress-related hormone to the fact that black women in their 20s were more likely to have maternal health problems than black teens. Over time, this stress hormone is released in the body and contributes to long-term health issues.[9]

Birth can be a stressful experience for any woman. Even if we are aware of our birthing rights and choices, it can take a lot of time and energy to express our wishes for childbirth. Though my births were challenging, I can't imagine having the added stress of racial discrimination.

Serena Williams's story and the experience of many women in the United States reveal the racial and ethnic disparity that still exists not only in our healthcare systems but in many of our social systems. The trials and sufferings of all women and children are our responsibility—whether we choose to do something about them or we turn away and nurse our own aches instead.[10] The nursing of our own aches and the fear of our own suffering can come at the detriment of others. When we refuse to look at our own biases and bigotries, when we don't take stock of our own fears or we support work that is only good for our health but not the health of all women, then trying to avoid our own deaths can often end up killing others.

17

CONQUERING NATURE

My first year at graduate school in Scotland, I walked the path beside the North Sea every day to get to class in the village. Some days the tide was up to the bank, and wet-suited surfers would brave the wind and fury of the sea. Other days, the water seemed to have forgotten the shore, and it lagged serenely beyond the beach. Some quiet nights when I walked home in the darkness, the full moon stretched out across the horizon of the sea and touched the water, and the whole earth seemed to listen and watch more closely. The haar, a heavy mist from the sea, would roll in and settle onto the village, onto the creek and the trees that populated my cemetery walks.

I'd never lived in such close proximity to the sea until I lived in Scotland, nor had I spent so much time walking in the darkness, especially a darkness that was so far away from the glare of city lights. I was becoming acquainted with the earth for the first time, and I began to really care what happened to it.

My relationship with the earth and the seasons deepened when we lived on a farm in Illinois. I was awakened by the created world, and as much as one can know a place in eight years, I began to notice the intimate details of our acreage. They changed and were refashioned by the seasons and the weather: the spot where the pokeweed always grew by the side of the cow pasture; the place up the ridge from the creek where stinging nettle grew wild and fast; the sandy bank down the creek under a fallen tree that was perfect for camping; the damp soil under the bluebells where we might or might not find morels. These places were beloved because we knew them and had seen them grow and had been changed by them.

For most of my upbringing, earth care was viewed as the domain of hippies and liberals—both inherently secular, of course—and not the concern of good Christians. I'd certainly never considered that the Bible might have anything to say about caring for the earth. For a lifelong churchgoer, my first experience with the Bible's wisdom on ecology came during a biblical studies class I took in graduate school that first year.

In the story of creation in Genesis, matter itself obeys the breath of God. God speaks, and the universe explodes, not into chaos but into the unique and glorious order of one who is all things creative: artist and scientist, mechanic and architect, master builder and painter. In Genesis 1:28, after creating humans, God commands them to "fill the earth and subdue it." Though I never explicitly heard the message that this command meant we should ravage the earth, the implicit understanding was that we were in charge. If we are supposed to subdue the earth, as the Bible clearly said, it made perfect sense that, as the center of God's creation, humans could take from the earth what we needed, using the earth's resources for our benefit.

It's true that the Hebrew word for *subdue*, when used by itself, can paint a disturbing picture of submission, of ravaging and stomping and overcoming. When read alone, those verses can and certainly have been used to promote a human overtaking of nature.

But the whole story of creation and God's relationship to all creatures isn't confined to the first chapter of Genesis. Chapter 2 describes a curious and relational God who places humans as helpers of both each other and God. It emphasizes stewardship and relationship. Humans, with God's direction, are essentially the custodians of God's creation.[1] Humans certainly hold a special place in creation, but their unique position requires humility, gentleness, and ultimately—as the New Testament commands—love. God's command to humans requires them to experience and love nature in order to know how to care for it. For how can anyone care for nature in any way without coming to know and love it? Without walking in the darkness and seeing the magnitude of the stars; without growing an heirloom tomato from seed; without walking a path through the woods or seeing the sunset over a flat desert expanse.

Theologian and activist Randy Woodley probably wouldn't be surprised that my experience of creation changed my knowledge and heart about earth care. "In the Native worldview," he says, "a person who knows mostly theory is considered to know very little; and most of what means something to American Indians cannot be learned in books. . . . In the Indian world we *experience*; in the Euro-American world we *gather facts* about it."[2]

I am a product of a culture that has been influenced by Enlightenment rationalistic thinking and ideas that date back to ancient Greece. The United States was birthed into the "toxic atmosphere" of a dualistic culture that viewed matter as evil, that separated the body and the spirit.[3] Woodley invites a distinction between this dualistic worldview and another, one that is holistic. In a holistic worldview (a worldview shared by many indigenous peoples), "all of creation (the material world) is considered both good and spiritual."[4] This holistic view is also God's view of creation in the first chapters of Genesis. God is the one who first calls creation good. There is not one element of creation that God leaves out of that description.

***

When Matthew and I lived on a farm, we had both long been convinced about our biblical mandate to care for the earth, and we wanted to live out our ideals. We were inspired in the earth care movement by the likes of Wendell Berry and Barbara Brown Taylor, and we loved caring for the earth on a farm.

But farming sustainably became an increasingly difficult way to make a living. For years, my husband put all of his energy and time into raising grass-fed beef and growing berries and vegetables with minimal pesticides. He and the other members of the farm team would attend big organic farming conferences that pumped them up for farming sustainably, and then they would go back to their farms and see the profit loss, and all the hours spent tilling the earth would feel depressing. It was a losing battle for him and for many of the people we knew who were trying to make a living running farms that offered healthy food with sustainable, earth-friendly practices.

Instead of being directed toward sustainable farms, our modern food industry prizes "feeding the world" with big factory farming, which requires farmers to rent or purchase more and more acres to make enough money in the large-scale production of corn and soy to pay off the debts of the giant machines needed to manage the fields. This means meat industries that raise animals in cramped and filthy conditions. It means chickens that are bred to have larger breasts for meat—so large that their legs break, no longer able to hold up the weight.

They are bred for death instead of being free to live a good life.

Caring for the earth has become increasingly difficult. The pesticides and chemicals we pump into the soil and the food we feed to animals are bad for their bodies and for ours. Scientists say these chemicals have also contributed to greenhouse gases, which warm the planet by trapping heat. In the last 150 years, the activities of humans have been responsible for nearly all of the increase in the atmosphere's greenhouse gases. The United States Environmental Protection Agency reported that in 2017, 9 percent of greenhouse gas emissions were derived from agriculture, from what we put into the soil, the ways we treat our animals, the ways we dispose of their waste.[5]

As a result of these greenhouse gases, lakes are shriveling, deserts are expanding, and islands are disappearing.

The heat of the warming planet melts ice sheets in Greenland and the Antarctic into the oceans. Within this century, sea levels are expected to rise as much as four feet.[6] And every year, the worsening effects of climate change displace an average of twenty-four million people by the effects of storms and drought.[7] They have been called "climate refugees" or "environmental refugees."[8]

Theologians who are paying attention to climate change have said that our looming disaster is not morally neutral. Pastor A. J. Swoboda says that "global surface temperatures, species loss, rising sea levels, loss of drinking water—these ecologic tragedies are a direct result of human sinfulness."[9]

Between Hawaii and the Philippines, the Marshall Islands are a chain of coral and volcanic islands that house seventy thousand people. Most Americans don't realize that these tiny islands are disappearing because of rising sea levels. We don't know that many residents must daily haul out the sewage and seawater that flood their temporary barriers.[10] We don't know that residents have had to watch the bodies of their buried loved ones wash out to sea when their coastal graveyards flood.[11] Some of the Marshallese might be saved because they are allowed to emigrate to the United States. But their homes will likely disappear within the next generation.

What does the destruction of the environment have to do with the fear of death? A lot, actually.

In the 1970s, Ernest Becker wrote on our mortality fears in his book *Escape from Evil*, in which he argued that our denial of death induces us to "assure the complete triumph of man over nature."[12] The Ernest Becker Foundation had this to say about Becker's prescient views:

> Nature is riddled with reminders of our corporeality, so maintaining order and control over nature creates the illusion that we can avoid death. We extend power over nature through heroic feats of science, technology, and economic growth. We cut our grass and fill our shopping carts to set ourselves apart from nature, which allows us to feel as though death is escapable. As Becker warned, immortality driven consumer desire, unfettered materialism, and exploitation of nature carry a dark underbelly: environmental destruction.[13]

Becker's warning is that our fear of death manifests itself in an attempt to either conquer nature or set ourselves apart from nature. We separate ourselves from nature because if we get too close to the earth, we might see the cycles of life and death inherent in the earth. We might notice the change of the seasons, the death of animals, the dormancy of plants. The closer we are to nature, the more we see that every living thing dies. And that reminds us of our own death. And, of course, the inverse is also true: the more disconnected we are from the earth, from the way it is itself a part of God's creation, the more we might be tempted to think that climate change doesn't matter.

It's not that we are heartless. We see and care that others are hurting. But our comforts are too enticing: our prepackaged foods, our single-use plastic, our appliances and cars, our endless addiction to meat. We cannot see beyond these fleeting things and their effects. Our comforts are like analgesics, putting us into a stupor so we don't have to think about how our guzzling of resources affects God's creation. Discomfort reminds us of our eventual decay. We don't have to think about how it affects our bodies. And we don't have to think about how it affects other people.

Our obsessions with comfort can destroy the lives of others. The Marshall Islands are so far away, so small. We are so far from seeing its realities. The truth is that I only know about the Marshall Islands because my nephew was born there. It breaks his parents' hearts to think that he might not be able to visit his home of origin one day. The people of the Marshall Islands cannot deny the realities of climate change because their lives and their homes are being permanently changed by it.

***

Mystics have been talking about caring for the earth for a very long time. The most obvious figure, a precursor to the stereotype of the tree-hugging hippie, is Saint Francis of Assisi. Francis's hagiography is overflowing with his care for all of creation. He preached to the birds, made friends with a wolf, and wrote stunning prayers of solidarity with creation. The well-known Christian hymn "All Creatures of Our God and King" has echoes of Francis's "Canticle of the Sun":

> Praised be my Lord for our sister the moon, and for the stars, the which He has set clear and lovely in heaven.
>
> Praised be my Lord for our brother the wind and for air and cloud, calms and all weather by the which Thou upholdest life in all creatures.[14]

A century before Francis, twelfth-century German mystic Hildegard von Bingen also showed deep reverence for the earth through her writing. As the tenth child of her family and therefore a living tithe, Hildegard was dedicated to the church by her parents when she was very young. At the age of eight, she was sent to live with an anchoress named Jutta in a cell attached to an abbey. What must life have been like for a child like that, living in close quarters with a nun who had chosen a living death, much like Julian of Norwich? Death and the loss of her family and her childhood must've informed Hildegard's life as much as piety.

Despite the oddness of their arrangement, Jutta taught her well. Hildegard learned Latin, memorized scriptures and songs, and could play instruments.[15] Eventually, Jutta's religious devotion drew so many pilgrims that their anchorage had to be converted into a Benedictine convent. When Jutta died, the other nuns chose Hildegard, only in her thirties, to be their director.[16]

Hildegard's gifts were many. She was a musician, a composer, a visionary, a writer, a scientist, and a healer. When she was in her forties she began to write about her many mystical experiences, beginning in her childhood. In her intense visions, Hildegard perceived inside all things the concept of *viriditas* or greenness. *Viriditas* is a force that "represents the principle of all life, growth, and fertility flowing from the life-creating power of God."[17] Author Matthew Fox, who has written extensively on the mystics, says that he has noticed three sources of this concept of viriditas: the rich ecological beauty of her home in the Rhine Valley, her "surge of creativity," and Scripture.[18] Hildegard loved and knew nature and it defined the ways she saw all of creation and the ways she read the Bible. The psalmists' many metaphors of life as flowing streams and, conversely, the absence of God being felt as a dry weary land are full of this idea of God's presence as a green, powerful force.[19]

Hildegard's spirituality is "deeply ecological" as well as profoundly Christian.[20] In her concept of this greening life force, she shows a reverence for all of creation, which she finds both sacred and interconnected.[21]

It's important in our Euro-Western context, one that is often apart from nature and increasingly sees nature as something to be utilized and subdued, that we understand our views of God's creation are not the *only* views. Our culture profoundly influences the ways we have read the Genesis creation stories. In fact, Randy Woodley says that some "traditional Indians" see the Genesis narrative as the story of the fall of Europeans.[22] From that mythic perspective, Native peoples were still living in the paradise Eden of the Americas when European colonizers brought all kinds of evil: disease, war, enslavement, violence, and death. The Genesis creation story in this context is about "disequilibrium," Woodley says.[23] Instead of seeking to test or conquer nature, the Western world needs to seek healing. If creation is to heal in the ways that God hoped for Israel, we can listen to Woodley, Saint Francis, Hildegard, and other visionaries who call us to adopt a worldview that recognizes the interconnectedness of all creation with our Creator.

***

You might say that the fear of death is at the heart of our human flaws. In *The Slavery of Death*, Richard Beck says that the fear of death "produces most of the sin in our lives."[24] If death was brought to the world through the fall of humans in Genesis, then perhaps it makes sense that our fear of that death has led us astray from the beginning. It leads us to racism and environmental destruction, to greed and obsession with success.

In 1973 Professor Ernest Becker's book *The Denial of Death* was published. He died of cancer shortly after at the age of forty-nine and went on to posthumously win the Pulitzer Prize for the book in 1974. *The Denial of Death* became a classic treatise on the pervasive fear of death that disturbs, influences, and often masters the lives of human beings. From the outset of the book, he states: "The idea of death, the fear of it, haunts the human animal like nothing else; it is a mainspring of human activity—activity designed largely to avoid the fatality of death, to overcome it by denying in some way that it is the final destiny for man."[25]

Becker believed that often the things we do, particularly as nations and corporations, that seem altruistic and heroic can have "the paradoxical effect of bringing more evil into the world."[26] What he was getting at was that our fear of death so invades our psyche and behaviors that we don't always realize that the grand heroic things we do can actually create more damage.

Becker's greatest impact on social psychology was that he created "a science of evil. He has given us a new way to understand how we create surplus evil—warfare, ethnic cleansing, genocide. From the beginning of time, humans have dealt with . . . their shadow side . . . by projecting it onto an enemy."[27]

We've seen this fear projection throughout our journey through history: Jews were scapegoated during the Black Death and then massacred during the Holocaust, Native peoples were slaughtered, Christians killed other Christians, and Africans were enslaved by the millions.

All so that we could "clean up the world, make it perfect, keep it safe for democracy or communism, purify it of the enemies of god, eliminate evil, establish an alabaster city undimmed by human tears, or a thousand year Reich."[28]

Harsh words. It's no wonder that Becker has not had mass popularity. In his introduction, Sam Keen posits that this is because Becker makes us feel bad about ourselves. He "shames us with the knowledge of how easily we will shed blood to purchase the assurance of our own righteousness."[29]

Becker's words aren't particularly hopeful. If we are so steeped in the fear of death, how then do we stop ourselves from doing evil? It is really hard. Especially because, if Becker is right, we often do evil out of good intentions.

Becker died at a relatively young age. In a deathbed interview, he told Sam Keen that after seeing the interest in his recent *The Denial of Death*, he wished he could be around to witness all of the things that would come as a result of his work. One wonders if Becker had lived longer, would he have been more or less hopeful?[30]

If we are to carry on Becker's work, we have the chance to find a way to hope, even if Becker had a hard time seeing it. Our first step is to see the way that death fears infiltrate, rearrange, and emerge out of our lives. If it takes a lifetime to untangle, that's okay. It's a lifelong task. This is also where the mystics can help. They've been on the same wacky human journey as we have, encountering their own desperate need for rescue. And ultimately, the mystics do what the saints have always done for those who journeyed with them: point them to the source of all grace, forgiveness, and clarity. They open their hands out to the God who longs to save them.

That's the best place to start.

PART V

LIVING AND DYING WELL: WALKING THE PATH OF THE MYSTICS

18

A LONELY DEATH

My grandmother Mimi died in the middle of my father's cancer treatments. Months before, my sisters and mother had moved her into an assisted-living facility near my parents' house in Texas. My mother was well aware that my grandmother wasn't caring for her daily needs properly. But, for a time, Mom walked the delicate balance between respecting a loved one's wishes and trying to keep my grandmother from harming herself further. It was painful, and they attempted the move several times before my grandmother could accept her new living situation.

After that, her mental health declined. The last time I visited her in the tidy assisted-living apartment that my sisters had meticulously decorated with her favorite things to make her feel at home, I had two of my small children with me. The presence of my children seemed to agitate her. She wasn't always coherent. She would turn away and point to the birdhouse outside her window and talk about how she loved to watch the birds.

My youngest daughter couldn't keep her hands away from a breakable Chihuahua figurine that sat on a shelf beneath Mimi's television. Though neither Mimi nor my father shared many memories of my father's childhood, we all knew about Bambi the Chihuahua, their family dog. As Mimi's contemporary memories faded, Bambi was always there, a representation of all she'd lost and those who had left her behind.

A few months after our visit, my father texted me a photo. I tapped it open and gasped. The grainy photo was just a picture of Mimi's face: she was lying in her bed, her eyes closed, her skin pale and bone-colored, sunken into her cheeks so that her head looked more skeletal than alive. She died days later.

***

I loved visiting Mimi's house as a child: her spider plant lamp that magically turned on or off with a tap of a leaf, the plastic Dutch boy and girl who stood in a permanent magnetic kiss even when you tried to pull them apart, the mottled marble floors that were the perfect texture for sliding on sock feet, the music box that played the melancholy "Lara's Theme" from *Doctor Zhivago*, and my father's childhood room that was preserved in time.[1]

My grandmother's house was part warm hospitality and part museum to the dead.

Mimi was the youngest daughter of a West Texas farmer who grew up an hour south of Lubbock. She didn't love farm life, and I always sensed that, as the youngest by several years, part of her aversion stemmed from the fact that she'd felt left behind by her older three siblings to wallow in the dust and melancholy of her parents' chosen life.

As soon as she was able, my grandmother left the homestead behind. She was smart and sophisticated. She got her degree, married my grandfather, and enjoyed traveling and the life that came with his thriving radio business. Years later, she became a very successful businesswoman.

Though all of her siblings married, Mimi was the only one to have a child, my father. She took pride in my father, dressing him up in clothes and costumes that my sisters and I found in trunks after she died. The costumes were wrapped and layered in faded brown tissue paper that disintegrated when we touched it, tossing up dust like old sad memories into the air. One particular costume—a bright-green satiny thing that had black feathers attached to it—was from my father's tap-dancing days. I don't know what the costume was supposed to be, but we continued finding its remnants in the unpacking process, as if those black feathers were a through line of memories, reminding us of something we couldn't quite put our finger on.

My father's memories from his childhood were scant, or if he could remember them, he told them to us sparsely. He told most things sparsely. He held his emotions and thoughts with a stinginess that seemed in sharp contrast to his generosity in the other parts of his life: his wealth and the church he served.

My grandfather, though dead since 1964, still inhabited the house he and my grandmother built together in the 1960s. He lived in his old office file cabinets and furniture. In the black rolling office chair that had been his. In his beat-up car that sat in one spot of the four-car garage all the years I visited, rat scat visible through the windshield when we tried to peer inside, wiping away the dust with small hands, wondering how much that car would be worth if it had been cared for.

But it wasn't only my grandfather's death that could be felt throughout the house. Gradually, as her siblings died, my grandmother was left as the sole keeper of her family's history, the last one alive. Her closets were full of the carefully wrapped and preserved possessions of her sisters. After she died, we opened up old wooden trunks and found neatly wrapped baby clothes so old they were falling apart, gloves and jewelry, postcards and letters too numerous to count.

Death lived in every corner of that house, changing faces and shapes as you walked through the rooms. Death could be warm and cozy, full of nostalgia. Death could be an unacknowledged sadness, a pain no one admitted was there because they didn't really understand what it was. It could be an unformed shadow, tucked away in dusty corners with stacks of old books and a tiny organ that hardly worked anymore.

After she died, my parents took Mimi's body back to Lubbock where she was buried beside her first husband. They were finally together again.

***

I recently read about a woman in Japan named Mrs. Ito, who is in her nineties and the last of her family members left alive. She lives alone in an enormous apartment complex in a sea of other identical apartment complexes that house other elderly tenants like her. She is afraid to die alone, so she's made a deal with a neighbor who watches for her curtain to open every day. "'If it's closed,' Mrs. Ito told her neighbor, 'it means I've died.'"[2]

Mrs. Ito's fear of dying alone isn't unfounded. Thousands of people die each year in such complexes in Japan, and no one finds them for days, weeks, or even years. Often they are found only when the stench becomes bad enough that their neighbors call the authorities to complain. One of the worst cases made international headlines: a man had been dead for three years in his apartment. He was only found because his automatic payments had run out and the authorities came looking for him. All that was left was a skeleton.[3]

There's a Japanese term for this phenomenon: *kodokushi* or "lonely death." A profession has risen up around these lonely deaths: people who come and clean up afterwards.

While the issues that led to this rash of lonely deaths in Japan are said to be an aftereffect of economic changes from the 1960s,[4] the truth is that loneliness and death are becoming increasingly associated all over the world.

Loneliness is at epidemic levels in the United States. Researchers at Ohio State University and West Virginia University (in states that have both been hit hard by the opioid epidemic) concluded that deprivation (high poverty, low education, and low employment) and loneliness are two of the correlations with suicide, which is the tenth leading cause of death in the United States.[5]

An opinion piece in the *New York Times* in 2018, "How Loneliness Is Tearing America Apart," talks particularly about how our divided political climate has been exacerbated by our social isolation. But what the piece also says is something that many of us are starting to understand:

"Most Americans suffer from strong feelings of loneliness and a lack of significance in their relationships. Nearly half say they sometimes or always feel alone or 'left out.' Thirteen percent of Americans say that *zero* people know them well. . . . Loneliness is worse in each successive generation."[6] That means that over thirty million people in our country don't have an intimate relationship in which they feel known. People are utterly lonely, and by all indications, they are lonelier than they've ever been.

I wonder if my grandmother Mimi was inherently lonely, if she had so suppressed the pain of the deaths and loss she'd experienced that she displaced her pain and fear on the trinkets and clothes and things she kept. She wouldn't be alone in doing this. I find myself holding onto things, whether they are material things or habits of mind, because they comfort me. Maybe like the people of the sixteenth century who reassigned their death anxiety from the skull to the passage of time, these things she kept became the tangible markers of her memories of the family members who had left her alone in life and then in death. Maybe they comforted her in her loneliness, in the feeling that had haunted her since childhood on the West Texas farm.

Living for eight years in intentional community gave me a unique perspective on the loneliness that pervades our culture. Many of us who are drawn to intentional community recognize our cultural isolation. We've been lonely, and we are desperately tired of it. So we seek out new family because our family of origin has broken apart or failed to nurture us properly. Or maybe we don't fit into the model of family that our churches have idolized: wife, husband, and children. We want family, too, even if it looks different. Intentional community, at its best, offers family and community in a more intensive way than most of us are used to.

Even if you didn't like every person in your community, local neighbors, family, and religious institutions used to function as community builders. Americans, as a whole, have lost trust in all of these institutions. We don't trust our government or politicians, we've moved away from our families, we've been hurt by our churches, and we increasingly lack trust in our neighbors.

When death arrives, if we are so disconnected from the people who used to offer connection and community in death, where does that leave us? If so many of us are without intimate relationships, then we are left with no one to talk to about death and no one to be with us when we die.

It's no surprise, then, that death aids have arisen in many unique places. Hospice care workers have provided end-of-life care to families for decades. But with our disjointed communities, more people are not only dying alone—they have no one to help them work through their fear of death. A new trend has arisen in contemporary alternatives to end-of-life care: death doulas or death midwives.

Death doulas perform many functions. Like birth doulas, they help families walk through the confusions and complications of healthcare options. With death doulas, however, most of their clients have a terminal illness. They also encourage an openness in talking about death, helping family members with difficult conversations so that death doesn't leave behind lots of regrets.

The International End of Life Doula Association says that among other things, doulas "help restore sacredness to dying."[7] One death doula explains that her task is to encourage people, in death, to "rely on each other" and not on institutions.[8]

The odd thing is that one of the "institutions" many Americans don't trust anymore, the church, wasn't just an *institution* but was full of the community of people who would perform these functions. Religious institutions have also been the locus for recapturing the sacredness of death.

I appreciate death doulas, their function, and the ways they serve people at their most vulnerable. But I have to admit that it saddens me that death doulas are even necessary.

People are desperate for a spiritual connection to death because they are no longer associated with communal spaces that used to offer this connection. With the loss of trust in the institutions that—however imperfectly—used to offer these things, death doulas are claiming a space that has been left empty. Ultimately, death doulas are attempting to help their clients imagine and enact their own version of a good death, the best death they can hope for.

19

GRIEF

My father battled cancer for two years.

Isn't battling a flawed metaphor for something over which we have very little control? *Battle* connotes strength on either side, a fight between armored, weaponed equals, following at least some rules of war, even if the reality of war is brutal. Maybe chemo or radiation or the surgeon's hands are strong enough opponents. Battling cancer, for all of its war overtones, feels more like a euphemism that offers a semblance of control to the ones in the company of such an illness.

We have come up with all sorts of euphemisms for death too. You're not likely to hear a death announcement with "He's pushing up daisies now" or "She kicked the ole bucket." Instead, you might say that a person "passed away," "departed," "is resting in peace," or "is in a better place." Even in church, we tend to use euphemisms when announcing a death. Instead of saying "he died," most often people say that a person "went to be with God" or was "called home."

Euphemisms soften the bluntness of something that's often too painful or taboo to talk about in polite company. We use euphemisms most commonly for body parts, for excrement, for sex, and for death, the things we don't like to talk about publicly.

In poetry, the sounds you choose to use at the end of a phrase are important for the context of the poem. The word "died" is a harsh-sounding and final word that goes well with its subject matter. We often don't want to say or hear the word "died" because it sounds too absolute, too definitive.

These euphemistic phrases are regularly used to comfort or offer spiritual hope. In some ways, they let us stave off the reality of death for a little longer. And maybe that's okay. Maybe some of us need that comfort, if only to give us a little breather before the real work of grief begins. Grief cannot be euphemized away. Even if you ignore it, grief will find a way to emerge out of the depths.

***

In his book *The Problem of Pain*, written in 1940, C. S. Lewis discusses the theology of evil and suffering, arguing that suffering is not enough of a reason to reject God. But when his wife died two decades later, his grief, doubt, and pain were so raw and so unlike the intellectual sureties of his other writings that his seminal work *A Grief Observed* wasn't published until after his death, and even then under a pseudonym.

I was in college taking a Bible course on the works of C. S. Lewis when I first heard this contrast of his two books on grief. In my black-and-white mindset at the time, I found it disconcerting that Lewis, considered a giant of the faith in my church tradition, doubted his faith. How credible is our belief system, I wondered, if such faithful members doubt and question when the going gets tough?

I didn't really understand grief or faith then. I didn't understand that if suffering made me question my faith, maybe it was not God who was the problem but my constructions of God or the theology I'd been taught. That's not to say that suffering always has a purpose. Maybe sometimes it just doesn't. Tell the father who has lost his three-year-old son in a freak accident that his suffering has meaning.

Actual pain and suffering often break us open so that we are no longer sure, no longer certain of our balance in the world, of our theologies, of the God we thought we knew. Our deepest beliefs, even the ones we wouldn't say aloud, are drawn out of us, displayed for us so that we see what convictions have lodged deeply in our hearts. Maybe we realize that we really believed all along that God would take care of us if we did all the right things. We see that deep down we thought God would reward our faithfulness by not letting anything bad happen to us. God would take care of everything for us.

Death can do such a number on us: it can feel like losing faith, like a painful breaking. It can feel like a flaying.

***

Even before he got sick, emails were my father's preferred method of communication. Email exchanges with him could be maddeningly brief and cryptic, something I'd often brushed off as a quirk. But it was even more pronounced when he got cancer. In the emails he sent to our family, the language was clinical. He would forward us his email exchanges with his oncologist and surgeon with very little commentary, leaving us to suss out the medical language.

My dad called his condition "adenocarcinoma" or a "disorder," refusing to use the term *cancer*. I don't know if this was because *cancer* was too imprecise—it meant too many things and therefore too little. It's true that the word *cancer* signified death to the rest of us. Perhaps that was the reason my father preferred the medical term. *Cancer* was too stark, too real, too final, and too full of a meaning that he didn't want to entertain. Even though it was the clinical term, I wonder if *adenocarcinoma* was actually my father's euphemism for cancer.

Before one of his procedures, I flew to Texas to be with him and stayed at my sister's house in the same town where my parents lived. My mother was with my dad in another city at a hospital that specialized in his kinds of cancer treatment, a two-hour drive from where they lived. Even though I could've driven up to the hospital easily, my mother urged me not to come. My father wanted his privacy.

In the week I was in Texas, having traveled so far to see him, I never did.

A few months later, Matthew and the kids and I flew from Illinois to Texas for Christmas. I was pregnant with our fourth child. Over the vacation, my father, who had been home for months, entered the hospital. We sat with my mom at home while she made the painful decision to put him in home hospice care.

The day he came home from the hospital was excruciating. My sisters and I had never seen our father so vulnerable. I think he would've preferred that we stayed away, the way I had stayed away from the hospital. He didn't want us there to watch as he was wheeled from the ambulance into my parents' kitchen. The doorway to their guest room was too narrow to wheel the bed in, so he had to get up, standing in the kitchen in his flimsy hospital gown, the pain so great on his spine that he groaned and gasped.

We turned away to give him privacy. Our strong, controlled father couldn't hold it all in anymore, and it was wretched to see his misery.

***

The last time I saw my father alive, he was lying in a hospice bed in my parents' guest room.[I] The television in the room had been playing a continuous loop of news most days since he'd arrived home. It made the room feel crowded and emotionally dull. Maybe that was the point.

That moment, like many memories, is both fiercely focused and hazy: I think that the television was on when I came into the room to say goodbye that morning. Maybe he muted it for those few moments. He didn't say goodbye in any conventional way. Or maybe there isn't a conventional way to say goodbye. Maybe saying goodbye was an admission that he wasn't ready to make, to finally accept that he was dying.

For all that I wanted him to cry in my arms, to weep that he loved me, I didn't want it either. I knew he didn't want me there for long, not because he didn't love me, but because, of all the people in his life, his daughters presented the most danger to him. Loving our children makes us vulnerable; it makes us weak and open to losing control.

Instead, he prayed over me and my growing baby.

When I first thought about that prayer, I thought about it as a gift. My theologian father, a man steeped in the Bible all of his life, gave me the gift he knew how to give. He offered me his best: a prayer, a theological reflection, an offering to God.

And maybe that was his best. But the other painful truth is that I think the prayer was a filler too. He felt awkward. He didn't know what to say or do. He didn't know how to say goodbye. So he fell back on the things he knew, those theological phrases that were easy for him. The words of prayer were easier to him than emotional truths.

I wanted him to do the hard thing. I wanted his heart and not his theology.

Because the truth is, our hearts express more of our theology than our words ever will.

***

My dad died in early February, with the light squeezing in through the slats of my parents' guest bedroom blinds. The cancer had crept up his throat so that he couldn't swallow, and his saliva had to be suctioned out of his mouth every few hours. Lumps began to emerge along his jawline in the last weeks of his life, the bulges of tumors that no longer hid inside his throat and along his spine. It was a horrible ending; and we were thankful when it was over. Now I see that it's much softer to say he "passed away," that "his battle was finally over," than to say we were thankful that he died.

I was home in Illinois that day, returning from a grocery store run. Matthew was waiting for me when I got back. He shuffled the kids over to our neighbor Angela, who was waiting at our door. Then Matthew gently grasped my upper arms. "Your father just died," he said and held me while I cried. I'm glad he was the one to tell me.

Maybe it was because I was so far away that almost immediately, I had a relentless desire to be with my father's body. I wanted to touch him, to know if his hands would still be as soft as they always had been. As his muscles stiffened, I wondered, would his face change quickly? As his blood settled down into the lower parts of his body, now that his heart had stopped pumping, would he smell any different?

Instead, I had to settle for a video chat. And the internet gods were cruel that day. Not only could I *not* touch him, I could hardly even see his body. Our farm internet swam lazily through cables that had been strung up by hand across trees and poles from the barn a mile away. As the video sagged and shifted, I caught images of my father's body, pale and smooth in his bed. My sisters sat together in a room that was cramped with family, watching over his body in a way I wanted to, communing over his corpse.

I couldn't smell him or touch him. I couldn't lay my fingers over his and cry. They showed me his hands on the video, and I heard snatches of their voices before the internet blanked out.

This was grief, I realized later: emotions that couldn't

be controlled, images and snatches of things that felt far away. Helplessness and frustration. Cursing softly as I felt the final disconnection, the final break in the line.

***

We soon embarked on the twenty-hour drive to Texas and made it to my parents' house at dinnertime, where my mom, sisters, and their husbands were waiting for us. Casserole dishes from my mother's church friends were stacked up in the fridge; baked chicken, mashed potatoes, and carrots were laid out on the counter. Her loving community had arrived in full force, and I felt like stuffing my face.

After we ate, the family gathered in my parents' living room, in much the same configuration that we'd had when my father first told us he had cancer two years before.

The rest of my family had all been together already, talking, planning, and grieving, but I was tired. And when they wanted to know how I was feeling, I couldn't answer.

Instead, the conversation turned to funeral plans. My brother-in-law distributed copies of my father's service plans, the ones my father had meticulously laid out for us. My dad had written two outlines for reflections he wanted specific people to give—all men. What we had was two or three mini-sermons, and no room for us, his family. His notes and reflections were intellectual and theologically correct, just like my father. They were also emotionally distant, just like he was too.

They felt clinical in their lack of care for the ways we

would need to grieve. They were focused on Christ, on the church: a good thing, for sure. But almost entirely devoid of heart.

If we, his three daughters, were going to be able to speak about our father, I realized that with three sermonettes, the funeral was going to be long.

And I couldn't stop thinking about it.

The nights before the memorial and graveside service, I slept fitfully in my childhood bed, tossing and turning, troubled. I became fixated on how long the memorial service would be, worried that people would grow restless and be annoyed.

I told Matthew this after a disturbed night of sleep.

"This should be the least of your worries," he said. "If anything, we should take our time honoring your dad and grieving. People who will travel from far away to be here won't mind having a longer service."

He was right, of course. But in reality, it would take intentionality to fight against the cultural stream that didn't know how to give us space to grieve.

***

The last few chapters of the book of Genesis are concerned with the death of the biblical patriarch Jacob (or Israel). Israel is surrounded by his family, particularly his sons and grandsons, and he offers them blessings that read like prophecies, some of them strange and dark, full of predictions of wealth, war, and power. After he breathes his last breath, his son Joseph instructs others to care for him according to Egyptian custom: he is embalmed in a process that takes forty days. And though

Jacob was a foreigner in Egypt, the passage says that when he died, the Egyptians mourned him publicly for seventy days. That's more than two months of public mourning.

A few chapters earlier in Genesis it is Jacob who mourns when he believes that his son Joseph is dead. Jacob tears his clothes, puts on garments of mourning, and refuses to be comforted for many days. In the Old Testament, mourning, loud and public, is an appropriate response to death.

In Yemenite-Jewish wailing culture, a culture that dates back to ancient times but is passing away in our contemporary age, wailers are chosen for their talent and ability to convey intense emotion. Professor of Anthropology Tova Gamliel describes wailing practices like this: "They shriek, abrade their skin, and gesticulate dramatically. In the least elaborate form of the wailing performance, they content themselves with a song of pain and loss, i.e., they make sounds and produce words accompanied by measured bodily movements."[2]

Young women and children observe the wailing, done by women in the Yemenite culture, so that they take in the lyrics, tune, and physical demonstration of wailing from a young age. Wailing is a communal ritual, part of the fabric of the Yemenite culture. One Yemenite-Jewish participant explains the practice this way: "Wailing is really to help [the bereaved] and give the feeling that you've lost someone and that everyone cares. We share it with you. Not by shaking hands and kissing and saying 'we commiserate' in a lip-service way. Instead, you have to go in [be emotionally involved]."[3]

Emotional involvement in funeral rituals is common in many cultures. Grief is the inward aspect of the death experience that will take longer. But the public, outward mourning is necessary to allow a person to move forward in grief. Grief counselor Dr. Alan Wolfelt says that "To mourn is to be an active participant in our grief journeys. We all grieve when someone we love dies, but if we are to heal, we must also mourn."[4]

In traditional funerals in Iran, outward emotions are an acceptable and even expected part of the "survivors' right to grieve." Not only are loud wailing and throwing oneself across the coffin of a loved one acceptable public displays of mourning, but emotional restraint, especially when tears are appropriate, is considered unhealthy.[5]

The practice of hiring professional mourners is becoming popular in some Western funerals, though the oddness of the practice is probably less an indication of its actual oddness and more an indictment on our Western ways of mourning. Vocal public mourning is certainly rare in our contemporary Western culture.

In New York City in 2016, a couple of days after the anniversary of September 11, an artist named Taryn Simon constructed an art exhibition called "An Occupation of Loss" to capture the various ways people across the globe respond to grief. Her artwork explored the "empty spaces, private and public, that loss produces, and the chaos, ritual and ceremony that help people fill the void." For this particular exhibition, Simon sought thirty professional mourners from different countries as far flung as Burkina Faso, Cambodia, Russia, and Venezuela to occupy her art space.[6]

While the mourners at Simon's exhibition represented personal losses, there was also a communal aspect to the mourning. Mourners had a function within the community to "mark larger losses . . . like displacement or exile, in a cultural role that is part witness, part historian and part poet."[7] Wailers and mourners can act as our artists and poets, bringing our attention to the things we might be tempted to look away from, not to cause pain unduly but for the emotional health of the community.

One of the things Simon wanted to explore was the ways in which a culture grieves. "When you look at how a culture grieves," noted a professor on Simon's team, "you are looking at the core of that culture."[8]

If it's true that the way a culture mourns reveals its heart, we might be in trouble.

We might look back at the oddness of the medieval and Victorian eras and wonder at their approaches to death, how they sought to accept and confront and cope with it. But aren't we odd too? We who have forgotten or discarded so many of the mourning rituals that many cultures still practice today.

I would venture to guess that many of us aren't comfortable expressing loud vocal emotion in public. It might be the exception rather than the rule if you went to a funeral in a Euro-Western culture where more than one person was loudly wailing or rocking. But that is just what happens at funerals all over the world. When death comes, the trauma of grief unlocks emotions that we have long held close, our still waters are no longer calm, our instincts are rearranged, and our bodies cry out despite ourselves. It can be confusing, and if our culture doesn't leave space for such emotions, whatever they may be, we end up trying to manage unruly emotions. In American culture, this outward emotional display feels like a loss of control.

Suppressing our grief can be dangerous to our spiritual, emotional, and physical health. Suppressing our grief, favoring control over truthful feelings, pushing sorrow into the recesses of our subconscious, leaves us floundering.

Maybe depression in the midst of deep grief comes not only from our suppression of a tangible, loud mourning but also as a result of our isolation within that grieving. Though we must deal with our grief inwardly, we aren't meant to grieve alone. Just as the members of the wailing culture surrounded one another as they learned and taught in community, so we ought to surround one another—not only in times of grief but beforehand, so that when death comes, we have intimate relationships, we have people we can count on.

While there are pockets of cultures in the United States who have continued to practice communal mourning rituals, in general, our American culture has very little to offer the mourner beyond the funeral. This should not be so for Christians. Our religious text, the very book upon which our faith is based, is constructed on promises and guidance and the rituals that offer hope beyond death. We have an entire book in the Bible solely dedicated to grief.

***

The Book of Lamentations offers not only language for those who were suffering in Israel at the time but an imaginative vision of how to grieve. For the people of Israel, Lamentations offered a window into "the pain of survivors in the aftermath of the destruction of Jerusalem."[9]

"Wailing texts" like Lamentations work to combine "speech and weeping with evocative vocalism. Its contents are improvised stories that deal with the meaning of death and the loss associated with the deceased."[10]

A book like Lamentations can feel depressing, off-putting, or boring to read. There might be a reason that readers, many of them Christians, respond that way. Old Testament scholar Kathleen O'Connor says this is because our "United States' capitalist society" requires us to live in denial, even denial of our own despair. If we had the courage to face our denial of death, instead of allowing our wealth, power, and privilege to buffer us from it, our eyes might be opened to a different reading of Lamentations. O'Connor believes that the book of Lamentations itself can be a tool for Western Christianity, which often lacks the "imagination and daring" to unearth our despair, to lift it "into consciousness." Such a reading might be revelatory. Such a reading might bring to light "our exhausted spirits, our broken communities, and our violent relationships, home and abroad."[11]

***

Matthew told me recently that when he dies, he doesn't want me to go through the funeral home. "I want you to handle my body," he said with a little smirk.

Then we talked about how wonderful it would be if we knew how to do a funeral like that—in an actual home, with a simple coffin, where we could sit with our beloved's body and touch it and mourn and wail.

"If my body was laid out in the living room," Matthew

said, "people probably wouldn't need to say I 'passed away.' It would be clear: I was dead."

Maybe those euphemisms for death are prevalent not only because we need comfort but because our eyes are fuzzy when it comes to death. When a dead body lies in front of you, it's a clear-eyed reminder of the stark reality.

For all my talk, I am still a product of a culture that suppresses grief, that tells me I shouldn't be sad. My culture slides its corpses up into cold metal refrigerator trays; it pumps its dead full of toxic chemicals that not only harm morticians but seep into the soil and harm the earth.

My culture is afraid of death and the decaying body. And I am too.

The day after I arrived in Texas for my father's funeral, my mom asked me if I wanted to go to the morgue and see his body. He didn't want to be embalmed.

"I'll go with you," Matthew offered.

I wish I could tell you that I went, that seeing his corpse gave me a chance to grieve. But I didn't. I imagined the scene in my mind like a television crime drama: walking into the cold metal room, the mortician pulling back the sheet from his face, the gasp of shock. And I didn't want to do it.

Maybe I was afraid of seeing him, of seeing the natural decay of his body. For all my longing to be with his body when I was far away in Illinois, I knew that after so many days had passed, his features would be different. I didn't want to be in that cold place that only held death.

Death and grief are not allowed in polite society, at least not for very long. When they come out of their corners and hidey-holes, we only allow them because we don't have control. They are the true taboo offenders that have been euphemized in our culture.

But what if we looked at them straight on, if we used their real names, if we screamed and wailed at them? I wonder if that's part of the beauty of having a wake in a home. It sheds the imaginary separation between living and dying. It reminds us of the mystery inherent in these parts of our existence: the paradox that in the very place where death resides on a table in the living room, the *living* has been and will be happening. In that same place, we have feasted, we have loved, we have slept, we have laughed, we have sung, and we have died. Allowing death into the home, opening the door to grief, and allowing ourselves to lose control aren't weird or morbid choices. They are acts of hope.

20

A GOOD DEATH

One afternoon I came up to our bedroom to find Matthew crying with a book open on his lap. This is not a typical occurrence; if anyone is crying over a book, it's usually me. He'd just reached the epilogue of Paul Kalanithi's *When Breath Becomes Air*, the truncated memoir of a surgeon who wrote of his experience of dying when he was diagnosed with cancer. Paul's wife wrote the epilogue after his death.

I lay down beside Matthew on the bed and he began to read me some passages from the book. When he couldn't finish it through the tears, he pointed to the final paragraph, a passage that Paul wrote for his eight-month-old daughter whom Paul and his wife had decided to have, even though they knew he was dying.

Paul says to his daughter, "When you come to one of the many moments in life where you must give an account of yourself, provide a ledger of what you have been, and done, and meant to the world, do not, I pray, discount that you filled a dying man's days with a sated joy, a joy unknown to me in all my prior years, a joy that does not hunger for more and more but rests, satisfied."[1]

I lay back against the pillow beside Matthew and we cried together.

We cried for Kalanithi and his daughter and the loss his wife experienced. We cried because we have four children and couldn't help but think about leaving them behind in death. We cried at the thought of losing each other.

But I realized that my grief was about something else too.

As Paul embraced the process of dying, his wife says that he intentionally accepted a role and a posture that surgeons are often unaccustomed to. He accepted his loss of control and the accompanying vulnerability that came with that. Most poignantly, Paul "let himself be comforted."[2]

Paul's book was truncated because he died before he could finish it. But after reading those words, I realized my grief felt truncated too—unfinished, cut short because I wanted that posture from my father as he was dying. I wanted my dad to have been vulnerable like that, to have allowed us to comfort him.

Part of the complexity of grief is that we have expectations of the way our loved ones should die, what we hope they will say to us, how we hope or expect to feel. Sometimes we have to grieve our expectations of death and grief, realizing that, even if we hadn't thought much about it, we had expectations of what a "good death" looks like.

***

Every culture, generation, century, and people group has an image of a good death. The people of medieval times generally hoped to live long enough to be able to repent before they died. For some people, a good death means having lived a good life so that they aren't afraid at the end. For others, a good death is quick and painless, free from any preparation.

For many Americans, a good death has come to mean that they die at home. Dying at home, especially if one is dying of a terminal illness, means that the carers need to have the help of the hospice care system.

Our modern American hospice care system, which was transformed in the 1980s by Medicare,[3] owes much to the philosophies and work of two religious women: one Catholic and one Protestant. In the late nineteenth century, author Rose Hawthorne Lathrop, the daughter of author Nathaniel Hawthorne, became a nurse in her forties. Her work with patients in New York City gave her a tangible look at the terrible ways the poor often died. She opened a free care clinic and eventually an order of nuns, becoming their Mother Superior, Mother Alphonsa. To Mother Alphonsa, nursing was a ministry, a way to share the gospel with her patients without proselytizing.[4]

Informed by her faith and conversion to evangelical Protestantism in the mid-twentieth century, British nurse Cicely Saunders cultivated the modern idea of hospice care. After working as a nurse in a cancer ward and seeing the loneliness of her dying patients, she wanted to create a system of care that could focus on the suffering patients as they approached death. She wanted to address all parts of the dying process: "the physical pain . . . the emotional pain, the discomfort of being in a bed for so long, the loneliness, the loss of control of one's body, environment, and future."[5]

The work that Saunders and Mother Alphonsa did in caring for the dying was informed by their faith and their experience. They saw the suffering that comes when people aren't cared for, when they are alone or destitute.

Access to good medical care, particularly at the end of life, was an issue in the communities of Cicely Saunders and Mother Alphonsa. It's still an issue now. By all accounts, if given the choice, most Americans would rather die at home. The good news is that, for the first time since the early 1900s, more Americans dying of natural causes are able to die at home rather than at the hospital.[6] But caring for a terminally ill family member, even if you have some measure of medical expertise, is still mentally, emotionally, and physically taxing. The burden of caring for my father was heavy on my mom. She was able to have hospice care, but that care was limited and expensive and didn't always give him the pain management that he could've had in a hospice care facility. They had to train her to care for my father, and she was on call 24-7 for months. Caring for a terminally ill patient at home can be an enormous burden.

There is also a darker side of our medical approach to death. Despite the uptick in Americans being able to die at home, nonwhite Americans and people who don't have cancer are still more likely to die in a hospital or other healthcare facility than at home.

***

My father read George MacDonald's *The Princess and the Goblin* to us when we were young. In fact, that is the only book I remember him reading aloud to us. The grandmother character in many of MacDonald's books reminds me of my grandmother, Oneta. I miss her. I miss her more now than I did when she died thirteen years ago. I miss the way her crooked fingers moved. Sometimes, I can almost smell the powdery spice of her perfume as I leaned down to kiss her. I think I need her now more than I did then, now when my daughter reaches her preteen years and I fumble to tell her something—anything—wise. I think I need her to remind me what it feels like to be always wanted, always accepted, and always heard so that I can do that for my children.

My grandmother had a "good death," at least by my own limited standards. We surrounded her, in and out of the hospital and hospice care in her last days. Although we weren't with her the moment she died, she liked to hear us sing to her, she wanted us to be near.

Until my father died, I didn't realize I had my own expectations for his death, formed by my own particular set of imaginings and community and the theologies of my heart.

I wanted us to surround him with love and music, with words of gentleness and affirmation. I wanted what we had at my grandmother's death. But that wasn't what happened. He was alone, mostly by choice.

Grief over my dad is a complicated grief. I grieve that we, as his daughters, didn't get to have tender moments with our father. I grieve for my dad and what he lost, for what he could've known about love, humility, and vulnerability if he'd been able to embrace his painful loss of control and then embrace us fully, with all the ways that our emotions made him feel weak.

I miss my father when I read his one-line emails that say "I love you dearly" or when I remember the tender moments when he was able to emerge from his self-imposed isolation into the world of love that filled the home my mom created. I miss him when I can accept my own failures, when I can see that we are all caught up in our own desperate attempts to cope with death. Maybe we miss our loved ones when we are able to remember the ways they gave parts of themselves to us.

A good death doesn't just happen. It accompanies a certain type of life, a life in which we have practiced dying. If we really allowed ourselves to think about it, what would our hopes be for a "good" death? How do we hope our mothers, fathers, or grandparents will die? What do we wish for our own deaths?

***

There is a deep mystery at work in our dying.

My mother-in-law, Debbie, recounted the story of what happened when her own mother died. Matthew's grandmother Gigi was almost ninety when she went on hospice in the nursing facility where she lived. When they knew their mother was close to the end, Debbie and her sister kept vigil at their mother's side day and night.

They had fallen asleep in recliners on either side of Gigi when they were both awakened. They looked over at their mother and reached for her. Though her body was still warm, they both knew that she was dead. Debbie and her sister wondered at their simultaneous waking. Had they roused at the same time because something tangible had passed through the room when Gigi died?

Threads of life and spirit and love connect us invisibly, even as we feel the pain when they break. If poetry is a focus on the shape, meaning, and details of life, then being in the presence of death can be a place where we are all offered the painful gift of becoming contemplatives and poets. The daily rush of our lives is forced to stillness and quiet, and we watch the chest rise and fall, listening with desperate intensity for the sounds of the last breath, attuned to all the things going on that we can't see.

Our poetry and prayers can only capture what we observe at death. For those of us who are Christians, our faith is supposed to tell us something about death and the afterlife, but still, when it comes, many of us discover we have been afraid of this inevitable path the whole time.

If we've learned anything about death in our historical timeline, it is that death can come swiftly and unexpectedly. A thief in the night, a storm on the horizon, a plague from the sea. So if death can come swiftly, what is the point in thinking about a good death anyway? Could it have something to do with the ways we live?

Death comes for all of us. We will all die. We will lose those we love. So if we know the truth, how shall we then live?

***

When Ernest Becker wrote *The Denial of Death*, his outlook was a little bleak. He didn't offer a lot of hope for those of us stuck in our habits, our psychologies, our idiosyncrasies, phobias, and fears. How were we to move forward knowing that our lives were embedded in a culture that denied death and therefore caused so much pain and suffering? Still, Becker did offer two "fragile" ways we can move toward not destroying each other through our fears of death.[7]

One is to develop a communal hatred for something that isn't human, some great evil like "poverty, disease, oppression, or natural disasters." This is worth thinking about but cannot be fully fleshed out in this book. The second way sounds new, but actually, it is an old path, well worn by our ancient philosophers and mystics. Becker's other solution is to "practice dying."[8] By "cultivating awareness of our death" we begin to recognize our vulnerability, our weakness, and our powerlessness.[9]

Is it possible that death can become a spiritual discipline, one that, if practiced, can form and inform the rest of our days? Is it possible that if we practice dying, we will be freed from fear to live in new life?

Becoming accustomed to death can strip us bare. Our armor is gone, and any illusions of control have faded. This can either lead us to despair or to something greater: to something or some person beyond ourselves.

21

THE SPIRITUAL PRACTICE OF DYING

One evening in late January, nearly three years after my father died, Matthew and I invited our friends Mel and Steve over to have a death dinner. When I told some other friends about our upcoming gathering, all sorts of jokes ensued. No, we were not going to eat dinner with a dead body laid out on our table (although that's a funeral tradition in some cultures), nor were we going to paint our nails and eyelids black and enjoy the melancholy of despair (although that sounds kind of fun in an ironic way).

Matthew brought up the idea of a death dinner to me when he read about a nonprofit that aims to open up discussions with people around the subject of death and dying. Death over Dinner grew out of conversations in a graduate school class at the University of Washington called Let's Have Dinner and Talk about Death. In 2013, the teachers of that course, Michael Hebb and Scott Macklin, started a website and birthed a movement with a simple invitation: invite friends over to eat and talk about death.[1]

So that is what we did. We took the script that Death over Dinner offers and used it as an outline for our evening. But, because we were all interested in the spiritual aspects of death, we added some of our own thoughts and questions.

I did add a touch of morbidity to set the mood. I turned on a death playlist I'd been assembling for a year and propped up a picture of a skull that Matthew bought me for my birthday.

Our evening began with the usual dinner chitchat. Then we read part of a liturgy about loss. I don't think any of us were really scared to talk about death—we'd approached these kinds of conversations with Mel and Steve before—but none of us really knew what to expect.

Once we got started, what unfolded was a long, rich, and beautiful conversation about our experiences with death. We recalled how old each of us was when we first understood that we were going to die. We talked about what we each envisioned when we thought of a "good death."

Mel described the many deaths she'd faced in her life and what each of them meant to her. I began to see how we experience every death differently: depending on our age at the time and our relationship to the person who died. Our conversation lasted for hours, until our children were ready for bed and wouldn't be put off any longer. We ended by talking about our spiritual thoughts about death: what we would regret at the moment of death and how we saw the afterlife.

One of the things that struck me most about our death dinner was how truly comfortable we were in talking about death. Granted, I've been focusing on death for a long time, and writing a book about it has certainly desensitized me to the subject. But it was a deep and vulnerable conversation that helped us let down our guard with each other.

I even learned a few things about Matthew. They weren't things he'd been hiding from me, just thoughts that he might never have thought to share with me if it had just been the two of us talking about death. This is one of the reasons that we need community when we talk about death. Having intimate relationships is unique and necessary. But our approach to death, if it is to be healthy, needs to be done in a wider community where the wisdom of many can be shared and passed around, creating wider spaces for grieving.

***

In an episode of the television show *Parks and Recreation*, Leslie and April go to a performance art show put on by April's friend Orin, a young man who is always dressed in black and hovers on the fringes of their gatherings. When April and Leslie walk into Orin's art show, it's a disturbing array of death and farm life. One person is dressed as a chicken emerging from a life-size egg, another is a farmer chopping the heads off fake chickens, and still another is a cow whose intestines are spilling on the floor. Blood is everywhere. April tells Leslie that the show is "about death and the city" and asks Leslie her favorite part.

"The heavy-handedness," answers Leslie.[2]

Her line is said for a laugh because the performance art show is obviously an extension of Orin's consistently bizarre and morbid behavior.

Other than April, all of the main characters, even the most generous of them, consistently berate Orin when he is present, often telling him to "go away, Orin." He is an object of annoyance and disgust.

In a largely lighthearted show, Orin functions in the *Parks and Recreation* universe as a memento mori, the nagging reminder—despite all the hijinks and humor—that death and darkness are present. Quite clearly, the other characters don't like this reminder. They push it away the way they do Orin.

We all need our own memento mori. The ways we respond to those reminders might be an indication of how comfortable we are with our mortality. The spiritual practice of death is a memento mori, reminding us of our mortality.

But there is a difference between Orin's ways of death and the ancient mystics'. To practice dying in the way of the ancient mystics doesn't mean to wallow in the meaninglessness of death like Orin's cynical performance art show (although cynical performance art can certainly be interesting). It doesn't mean to live permanently in youthful angst, dressing in black and towing our black dog named Crow after us like the Italian artist Caravaggio.

In the Christian faith, death is not meaningless.

One of the reasons that my Christian faith is so important to me is because of the ways it interacts with death. As priest and scientist Jonathan Jong says, so many aspects of our faith "whisper *memento mori*."[3] Death flies through the story of creation: tempting, murdering, flooding, burning, warring, and sickening. Death thinks it has won when God gives up eternity for the love of us.

Audrey Assad's version of the song "Death in His Grave" has been on repeat in my house for the last year as I've written this book. I love the last words of the chorus the most: "The man Jesus Christ laid Death in his grave." When Jesus woke up on that Sunday morning, with breath and blood pumping through him, his eyes flashing open, what was the weight of that joy he felt? Knowing that he'd done it, that God had kept those promises. When he awoke, he broke through the fear of death, blowing it away like ash and dust. When he untangled himself from the burial clothes and laid them in the place where his body had been resting, he was also laying death in its place, burying it inside the tomb and leaving it behind him.

Of course, death would need to be buried and reburied until time was finished. But in that moment, death felt the first killing blow.

I need to be reminded that death is on its way out. But I also need to embrace the ways that death has been transformed. As we practice dying, we see how death has been transformed, not because everything is now okay but because death has been tricked into making us see life anew.

The experience of death is still sad. Death is still dancing us to our graves no matter who we are. But resurrection means that we are offered more.

Death isn't the end of God's story. It's not the end of God's incarnated story of Jesus or God's story of all created beings. Death isn't the end. We cannot be content to stop and live in a bland acceptance of the grief and darkness in the world. The spiritual practice of dying is an exercise in hope.

***

If dying is a spiritual discipline, then, like every spiritual discipline, it takes practice. We won't be good at it the first time or the second. We may never really be great at it at all. But just like those Day of the Dead celebrations in Mexico, or All Souls' Day, or the *Danse Macabre*, the spiritual practice of dying functions as a consistent reminder that we are all bones and dust, we will all return to the earth.

In the spiritual practice of dying, we acknowledge our eventual death. We look at how the denial of death has crept into our ways of living. We talk openly with our family and friends about what we hope for. We allow ourselves to mourn and grieve. We seek out community with others, inviting them to talk about death, whether we do it over dinner or not. We offer to be with other people in their dying.

One of the central reasons that we practice death is that it helps us love others. When our lives are preoccupied with our own comforts and health, with the things that will help us avoid thinking about death, we are focused on ourselves. If we are ruled by what Orthodox theologian John Romanides calls the "sway of death," then our neurotic anxieties overtake us, making us overly concerned with our own needs and unable to care for the needs of others.[4] Richard Beck says only by being emancipated from fear of death are we able to be "liberated from self-interest in the act of genuine love."[5] Facing our fear of death can help us love others better.

God offers to awaken us with death and resurrection. When I chose to enter into this story of resurrection, I was taught to die, too, to be drowned in baptism and be awakened to new breath. Like the mystics, I am asked to commit to the practice of dying to myself in order to take on God's life. What awaits us after that, whether in this life or the next, is total unity with the God who poured out everything for love.

Conclusion: Anointing the Grave

As I finish the final edits on this book, it is the Spring of 2020. Coronavirus (COVID-19) has emerged from the mysterious shadows of our mortal bodies and spread across the world, reaching our tiny corner of Ohio. Matthew and I have reworked our schedules so that I can finish this book, since all of my children are now quarantined at home.

What a strange experience, to be editing passages about plagues and corpses, about wakes and funeral rituals, about disruptions and death while our world suddenly becomes smaller because of a virus, our schools closed, our restaurants, libraries, and churches shuttered.

Terror sweeps through the swiftly changing news cycles, and we can't look away. Scientists have explained that because no one has ever had this kind of virus, none of us has the antibodies to fight the illness. Quite literally, no one is immune. Just as the Black Death sickened kings and bishops, the coronavirus has seemed to sweep through the halls of power and wealth, sickening celebrities and politicians.

However, things have changed a bit. Death itself might be the Great Leveler, but COVID-19 is not. As one journalist said recently, those who are "serving on the front line right now," healthcare professionals and those workers who are often in lower-paying jobs, "are more likely to catch the disease because they are more exposed."[1] None of us are immune to this virus, but some of us are more vulnerable to its worst offerings.

Marriage ceremonies are having to be rescheduled or rearranged. But most heartbreakingly, even in our own church community, funerals have been postponed, not because clergy are dying the way they did during the Black Death but because no one can gather together in large groups. Our church members are aching to be with one another, to mourn with one another. And we cannot.

By the time this book is sitting in your hands, I do not know how different our lives and culture will be. What will occur in the coming months and years? Will people continue to express their fear of death with hatred toward those who are sick? Will they find a scapegoat? Or will we bring our best selves to this crisis and show grace and love to one another?

The prophets and mystics of our church are needed more than ever, offering a theology that cares for the body, for our neighbors, and for the earth, words that give truth but also offer the strong flames of hope in such a frightening time.

We are living in an eerie, often hazy boundary, much like the moments between sleep and waking when things cannot always be worked out.

These seasons when we feel vulnerable, when life has swatted away the stuff that we've used to fortify ourselves from the raw truth—these are important in the inner workings of the soul. Joan Chittister says that in these gaps, when our bodies and minds are raw and vulnerable, something awakens within the soul. "What we suppress in the light emerges clearly in the dusk. It's then," she says, "in the still of life, when we least expect it, that questions emerge from the damp murkiness of our inner underworld."[2]

The image itself, of the damp murkiness of the inner world, disturbs and draws me closer. Many of the mystics know this damp inner world very well. They have traversed this part of the soul, have written about its crags and peaks, its turrets and parapets, the way it can feel empty. They know that these are the times and places where the soul is willing to bend toward something new.

Perhaps we have created that space here as we've thought about death. We have broken down our walls and let our souls stretch out toward something new. We have resisted the urge to exit when the discomfort comes and takes a seat on that tilted cemetery bench.

As I reflect on this writing and the exploration of the fear of death, I wonder if my soul, too, has been awakened by death. You might say that being awakened by death means that my soul is in recovery. I am in recovery from the fear of death. My soul is healing.

***

The first time I was able to make it back to Texas to visit my father's grave, it had been two years since his funeral.

It was a June afternoon when I began the half-mile trek from my mother's house to the cemetery where he is buried. It was—obviously—a hot day (it was summertime in Texas). I didn't mean to wear black to express mourning. And wearing black turned out to be an unwise choice for this particular day. By the time I crossed the bridge that arches over a highway near the cemetery, I was breathless from the hot sun and humidity.

The old memorial park where my father is buried stretches out so far that once I walked through the gates, I was dismayed to realize that his grave was almost all the way back in the direction I came. As I got closer to my father's grave, I noticed a small graveside funeral going on just yards from his headstone.

Memories of his graveside service from two years ago came back to me. At the time of that service, I was six months pregnant with my fourth child, leading an intimate service that was not really what my dad would've wished. My mom and sisters and I had been annoyed that his insistence on control had reached out, ahem, from the grave.

He had planned his entire funeral service down to each tiny detail, and it didn't leave space for our grief. The graveside service offered a compromise. The day before the church funeral we could grieve in our own way.

I led songs that day in February with a guitar that barely fit over my pregnant belly. My brothers-in-law and nieces read Scripture. My mom insisted that the gravesite workers not lower the coffin down until we were ready. This must've been different to them because she had to repeat this request to make sure it was followed.

When it came time to lower the casket, I gathered with my mom and sisters around it. There is something so final about that moment, the lowering of the coffin. It's not as if we thought he would come back from the dead before then, but the truth of death became most visceral when his body was lowered into that hole. All our grief emerged. We tossed flowers, one by one, onto his coffin, spoke words to him and to each other, and wept.

I was reliving all of this when I finally reached his headstone in the Texas sun two years later. And I realized something. The last time I'd seen his grave, a tent had covered the whole area around it. But without that tent, I could see more clearly how my dad's black headstone was sitting at the edge of the road alone, apart from all of the other gravestones on his row. He was directly in the sun, unshaded by the beautiful old Texas trees in other parts of the cemetery. A small clump of fake flowers flapped around in front of his gravestone.

It was partly laughable that my dad was alone at the edges of the cemetery because that was what he chose to do in our family life too. It wasn't that he was a bad father—I know he loved us—but he was so often at the edges of our gatherings, flitting in and out as he wished, rarely allowing himself to be emotionally present.

But I didn't laugh at first. His headstone looked so sad and alone in the hot sun all by itself. I sat down on the grass over his grave and cried hot sweaty tears. And then I wished I'd brought him some flowers. I searched my backpack instead for something, any kind of memento to leave.

Here's what I found: bug repellent that I'd made from essential oils at home. So, I did what any normal daughter does: I anointed his grave with oil. At least it would keep away the bugs for a few hours.

When I was done, I searched my phone for a prayer. I found one by the thirteenth-century mystic Saint Bonaventure. Bonaventure was born in Italy about five years before Saint Francis of Assisi died. Legend says that Saint Francis actually healed Bonaventure from a childhood illness. The child Bonaventure grew and became a Franciscan himself, whose mystical writings and teachings are filled with compassion. Though I didn't know it at the time, this prayer of his reveals Bonaventure's warmth:

> Let us die, then, and enter into the darkness, silencing our anxieties, our passions and all the fantasies of our imagination. Let us pass over with the crucified Christ from this world to the Father, so that, when the Father [and Mother] has shown himself to us, we can say with Philip: *It is enough.* We may hear with Paul: *My grace is sufficient for you.* And we can rejoice with David, saying: *My flesh and my heart fail me, but God is the strength of my heart and my heritage for ever.* Blessed be the Lord for ever, and let all the people say: Amen. Amen![3]

After I spoke the prayer, I walked back home.

The next day happened to be Father's Day. I called my sisters, Elena and Heatherly, and we bought some plants at a nearby nursery to put in the ground to make his grave look a little less forlorn. One of them was called "Mystic Spires Blue Salvia," a Texas Superstar winner variety that can withstand the Texas heat and, hopefully, a little loneliness in the cemetery.

We dug into the hard ground, pulling a hose over from a neighboring spigot to soften the soil. We sprayed each other with water and we laughed. We told our father that we loved him and forgave him for what he was not. Heatherly gave him a little scolding that made us feel better: if he wanted to sit in the sun by himself for a few million years, that was his choice.

As we drove away, I told Elena that I finally understood why people returned to the graves of their loved ones. It might sound strange, but before my father died, even though I enjoyed cemeteries, I never thought much about visiting the graves of my loved ones. They weren't there anymore. What did it matter?

But those moments spent at my father's grave made me realize that in order to pass through our grief, we need contact with the tangible things that represent death, at least sometimes. Maybe we care for places of the dead because we know it is the last gift we can give to the people who have died. More likely, it is also for our own benefit, so that there is one place dedicated to a final, physical connection to our loved ones.

Our grief needs embodiment. That is why some people are returning to wakes and bathing the bodies of their loved ones. That is why some traditional cultures spent weeks in mourning, in physical tears and wailing, in feasting, and sometimes even keeping vigil with a decaying body.

That is why the mystics cared for the physical wounds of others. That is why people visit the graves of their loved ones, year after year. That is why Mary was headed to the tomb of Jesus when she met him in the garden. That is one of the reasons that resurrection is so important in the Christian tradition: because our God became embodied.

As you are about to end this book and go about your day or close it for the night and enter into the hazy space between waking or sleeping, recall what you have learned in those murky places in your life where the soul is open to growth. If you are ready to practice dying, begin now and fortify yourself for the coming tide of life and healing.

It will not be easy; there is often pain in the process of a spiritual renewal. But the longer we do it, the more we see that the practice of dying is a gift of love that illuminates the path toward awakening.

> Awake, sleeper,
> And arise from the dead,
> And Christ will shine on you.
>
> (Ephesians 5:14 NASB)

ACKNOWLEDGMENTS

Though the task sometimes involved anxious writing days, bad dreams, tears, and lots of desperate prayers, it was such a gift to be able to create this book. Most of all, it involved the care, support, and encouragement of many people. I would not have written this book at this moment if my editor, Lisa Kloskin, hadn't called me up and asked me for a pitch. Thank you, Lisa, for taking my proposal and walking with me through panicked emails and phone calls. Thank you to Rachel Reyes, Mallory Hayes, and the whole team at Broadleaf Books for all your beautiful work in bringing this book into the world.

The first draft of this book began a few years ago when I was raw to the world and open to facing death. I had the great fortune to pick up Richard Beck's *The Slavery of Death*, and my eyes were opened to this cultural fear. Thank you, Dr. Beck, for your good work. Thank you also to authors and academics like Dr. Brandy Schillace and Dr. Phoebe Spinrad, whose work I relied on for their rich historical perspective. Any mistakes are mine and mine alone.

When we moved to Ohio three years ago, the community of people at Midway Mennonite opened its arms to us, and it has never stopped supporting us. Thank you to everyone who has helped with childcare and meals, who made us cookies and birthday cakes, who taught our children and wrote encouraging notes, who didn't mind that our kids ran around the sanctuary, made lots of noise, and took off their shoes.

Thank you to Greg and Ellen Bowman for providing extra support and friendship and being a place of refuge for us and our children. To Ethel Wenger, for being a friend from the moment I met you, for literally sifting through my dirty laundry, and for sharing your heart.

Thank you to Lisa Schwartz and the Generations Coffee family for providing a comfortable and child-friendly place to work.

To my group of misfit women in Ohio who offered me friendship just when I needed it: Vicki Ritterspach, Esther Harsh, Mel Montgomery, and Elisabeth Nelson. To Mel and Steve Montgomery for not only listening to me talk about death but sharing your stories with us over dinner. Thank you to Lucy Montgomery for babysitting my kids over the summer.

To the woman who gave me her bracelet after one of my talks because she felt a mystical draw to do so: I wear it every time I give a talk. I am honored by the gift of those who have shared their mystical experiences with me.

Writing can be a desolate and frightening task. I'm grateful for the encouragement of fellow writers like Shawn Smucker and Ed Cyzewski who know the terror, loneliness, and joy of writing books about death and spirituality. Thanks to Jon Sweeney for offering me some initial direction about mystics who focus on death. Thank you to Lisa Deam for being an early reader.

Kirstin Jeffrey Johnson and Jennifer Trafton: thank you for your Hutchmoot talk on George MacDonald, which gave me a more holistic picture of this beloved man. Kirstin, thank you for all your wisdom on MacDonald, for quotes on death, and for directing me to Coleridge.

Jessica Mesman and the community of *Good Letters*: you gave me a place to write about death and the mystics before I knew what I was doing. Thank you for holding space for writing that doesn't fit anywhere else. I miss you.

To Angela Adams for being my sister in community.

To my group of writerly women who have offered essential thoughts on everything from queso, child-rearing, and edits. You have influenced my work in countless ways: Kelley Nikondeha, Danielle Mayfield, and Amy Peterson. With special thanks to Jessica Goudeau, for more than twenty years of friendship, and to Stina Kielsmeier-Cook for introducing me to Saint Francis de Sales.

Debbie and Craig Peterson, thank you so much for the ways you care for all of us.

To my mom and sisters, Heatherly and Elena, for always being my home even so far away. Thank you for letting me share my side of the story.

Thank you to Neva, Jude, Annalee, and Isaac for putting up with all this death stuff, for being excited about *Harry Potter*, for listening to our communal stories, and for teaching us with yours.

Matthew, so much of this book emerged out of conversations we've had but most of all from the griefs and joys we've shared in the last thirteen years. I'm so grateful for our love and partnership. What a gift to be able to live this life with you. You are truly my treasure.

This book is for anyone who is afraid of death, who has loved and lost, who didn't know how to grieve, who has found the courage to step outside cultural norms and mourn out loud. I hold you in my heart.

FURTHER READING

Beck, Richard. *The Slavery of Death*. Eugene, OR: Cascade, 2014.

Becker, Ernest. *The Denial of Death*. 1973. Reprint, New York: Free Press Paperbacks, 1997.

Boase, T. S. R. *Death in the Middle Ages: Mortality, Judgment and Remembrance*. London: Thames & Hudson, 1972.

Bostic, Joy R. *African American Female Mysticism: Nineteenth-Century Religious Activism*. New York: Palgrave Macmillan, 2013.

Bowler, Kate. *Everything Happens for a Reason: And Other Lies I've Loved*. New York: Random House, 2018.

Chittister, Joan. *Between the Dark and the Daylight: Embracing the Contradictions of Life*. New York: Image, 2015.

Cox, Michael. *A Handbook of Christian Mysticism*. London: The Aquarian Press, 1986.

Cutter, Mary Ann G. *Death: A Reader*. Notre Dame: University of Notre Dame Press, 2019.

De Sales, Saint Francis. *Consoling Thoughts on Sickness and Death*. Compiled by Père Huguet. Charlotte, NC: TAN Books, 2013.

Doughty, Caitlin. Ask a Mortician. YouTube Channel. https://tinyurl.com/oqgrn6x.

———. *Smoke Gets in Your Eyes: And Other Lessons from the Crematory*. New York: W. W. Norton, 2015.

———. The Order of the Good Death. https:// tinyurl.com/ 6vz8b82.

Dunbar-Ortiz, Roxanne. *An Indigenous Peoples' History of the United States*. Boston: Beacon Press, 2014.

Emling, Shelley. *Setting the World on Fire: The Brief, Astonishing Life of St. Catherine of Siena*. New York: St. Martin's Press, 2016.

Harper, Elizabeth. All the Saints You Should Know. https://tinyurl.com/txvwqbt.

Harris, Mark. *Grave Matters: A Journey Through the Modern Funeral Industry to a Natural Way of Burial*. New York: Scribner, 2007.

Hein, Rolland. *Christian Mythmakers*. Chicago: Cornerstone Press, 2002.

Hein, Rolland, ed. *The Heart of George MacDonald: A One-Volume Collection of His Most Important Fiction, Essays, Sermons, Drama, Poetry, Letters*. Vancouver: Regent College, 2004.

Huber, Emily Rebekah. *"Oh Death!": Death, Dying and the Culture of the Macabre in the Late Middle Ages*. Rochester, NY: University of Rochester Libraries, 2005.

Iserson, Kenneth V. *Death to Dust: What Happens to Dead Bodies?* Tucson, AZ: Galen Press, 1994.

Julian of Norwich. *Revelations of Divine Love*. New York: Penguin Books, 1999.

King, Ursula. *Christian Mystics: Their Lives and Legacies throughout the Ages*. Mahwah, NJ: HiddenSpring, 1998.

Kalanithi, Paul. *When Breath Becomes Air*. New York: Random House, 2016.

Laderman, Gary. *The Sacred Remains: American Attitudes Toward Death, 1799–1883*. New Haven: Yale University Press, 1996.

McGill, Arthur C. *Death and Life: An American Theology*. Edited by Charles A. Wilson and Per M. Anderson. Philadelphia: Fortress Press, 1987.

McGinn, Bernard, ed. *The Essential Writings of Christian Mysticism*. New York: The Modern Library, 2006.

Neumann, Ann. *The Good Death*. Boston: Beacon Press, 2016.

Partridge, Michael, and Kirstin Jeffrey Johnson, eds. *Informing the Inklings: George MacDonald and the Victorian Roots of Modern Fantasy*. Hamden, CT: Winged Lion Press, 2018.

Raeper, William. *George MacDonald*. Oxford: Lion, 1987.

Rolf, Veronica Mary. *An Explorer's Guide to Julian of Norwich*. Downers Grove, IL: IVP, 2018.

Schillace, Brandy. *Death's Summer Coat: What the History of Death and Dying Teaches Us About Life and Living*. New York: Pegasus Books, 2015.

Spinrad, Phoebe S. *The Summons of Death on the Medieval and Renaissance English Stage*. Columbus: Ohio State University Press, 1987.

Sweeney, Jon M. *The Enthusiast: How the Best Friend of Francis of Assisi Almost Destroyed What He Started*. Notre Dame: Ave Maria Press, 2016.

Teresa of Ávila. *The Autobiography of St. Teresa of Avila*. Translated by Kieran Kavanaugh and Otilio Rodriguez. New York: Book-of-the-Month Club, 1995.

Thurman, Howard. *Deep River and The Negro Spiritual Speaks of Life and Death*. Richmond, VA: Friends United Press, 1975.

Trent, J. Dana. *Dessert First: Preparing for Death While Savoring Life*. St. Louis: Chalice Press, 2019.

Truth, Sojourner. *The Narrative of Sojourner Truth*. Edited by Olive Gilbert. 1850. Facsimile of the 1884 edition, with an introduction and notes by Nell Irvin Painter. New York: Penguin Books, 1998.

Twiss, Richard, *Rescuing the Gospel from the Cowboys: A Native American Expression of the Jesus Way*. Downers Grove, IL: IVP, 2015.

Woodley, Randy S. *Shalom and the Community of Creation: An Indigenous Vision*. Grand Rapids: Eerdmans, 2012.

Wright, N. T. *Surprised by Hope*. London: SPCK, 2007.

Notes

Introduction: Graveyard Meditations

1. Howard Thurman, *The Negro Spiritual Speaks of Life and Death*, in *Deep River and The Negro Spiritual Speaks of Life and Death* (Richmond, VA: Friends United Press, 1975), 11.
2. Shane Claiborne, Jonathan Wilson-Hartgrove, and Enuma Okoro, *Common Prayer: A Liturgy for Ordinary Radicals* (Grand Rapids: Zondervan, 2010), 271.
3. Joy R. Bostic, *African American Female Mysticism: Nineteenth-Century Religious Activism* (New York: Palgrave Macmillan, 2013), xvi.
4. Bostic, xvii.
5. Bostic, xviii.
6. Bostic, xviii.
7. Shelley Emling, *Setting the World on Fire: The Brief, Astonishing Life of St. Catherine of Siena* (New York: St. Martin's Press, 2016), 25.
8. Bostic, *African American Female Mysticism*, xiv.
9. Michael Cox, *A Handbook of Christian Mysticism* (London: The Aquarian Press, 1986), 42.

10. Cox, 42.
11. Cox, 40.
12. Kenneth V. Iserson, *Death to Dust: What Happens to Dead Bodies?* (Tucson, AZ: Galen Press, 1994), 516.
13. Iserson, 517.

CHAPTER 1: THE GREAT LEVELER

1. Sharon N. Dewitte, "Mortality Risk and Survival in the Aftermath of the Medieval Black Death," *PLOS ONE* 9, no. 5 (July 2014): https://doi.org/10.1371/journal.pone.0096513.
2. Editors of Encyclopaedia Britannica, s.v. "Black Death," *Encyclopaedia Britannica*, last updated December 13, 2019, https://tinyurl.com/y835fvra.
3. Phoebe S. Spinrad, *The Summons of Death on the Medieval and Renaissance English Stage* (Columbus: Ohio State University Press, 1987), 1.
4. Marian Massie, "The Dance of Death and The Canterbury Tales: A Comparative Study" (master's thesis, North Texas State University, 1973), 34–37, https://tinyurl.com/rcj9dxe.
5. T. S. R. Boase, *Death in the Middle Ages: Mortality, Judgment and Remembrance* (London: Thames & Hudson, 1972), 54–56.
6. Massie, "The Dance of Death," 2–6.
7. CNA Daily News, "Memento Mori – How Religious Orders Remember Death," *Catholic World Report*, October 30, 2017, https://tinyurl.com/yakx4h9y.
8. Spinrad, *The Summons of Death*, 13.

9. Spinrad, 30.
10. Spinrad, 30.
11. Jack Santino, "Halloween in America: Contemporary Customs and Performances," *Western Folklore* 42, no. 1 (January 1983): 7, https://tinyurl.com/st7gsyh. That's not to say that Christian missionaries wholeheartedly embraced Celtic practices. Missionaries called the gods of the Celts "demonic" and accused practitioners of witchcraft, sending them into hiding.
12. Santino, 7.
13. Brandy Schillace, *Death's Summer Coat: What the History of Death and Dying Teaches Us About Life and Living* (New York: Pegasus Books, 2015), 65–66.
14. Stanley Brandes, "The Day of the Dead, Halloween, and the Quest for Mexican National Identity," *The Journal of American Folklore* 111, no. 442 (Autumn 1998): 359–80, https://tinyurl.com/u53fduu.
15. Juan Pedro Viqueira, "La Ilustración y las Fiestas Religiosas Populares en la Ciudad de México (1731–1821)," *Cuicuilco* 14–15 (January 1984): 13, quoted in Brandes, "The Day of the Dead," 363.
16. Santino, "Halloween in America," 15.

CHAPTER 2: THE SPECTER OF AGE

1. Chloe Sorvino, "Why the 5 Billion Beauty Industry Is a Gold Mine for Self-Made Women," *Forbes*, May 18, 2017, https://tiny

url.com/sywgyxg.

2. Sangeeta Singh-Kurtz, "The Body-Positive Skincare Trend Is Driven by Women's Fear of Aging," Quartz, November 4, 2018, https://tinyurl.com/vfljppm.
3. Singh-Kurtz.
4. Chelsea G. Summers, "Aging Ghosts in the Skincare Machine: On Expensive Skincare and a Changing Face," Gay Mag, April 10, 2018, https://tinyurl.com/ry72foz.
5. Josephine M. Cummins, "Attitudes to Old Age and Ageing in Medieval Society" (PhD thesis, University of Glasgow, 2000), 130, https://tinyurl.com/udz32l7.
6. Cummins, 135, 137.
7. Cummins, 64.
8. Cummins, 76.
9. Cummins, 77.
10. Cummins, 82.
11. Cummins, 92.
12. Corinna E. Löckenhoff et al., "Perceptions of Aging across 26 Cultures and Their Culture-Level Associates," *Psychol Aging* 24, no. 4 (December 2019): 941–54, https://tinyurl.com/u47qwcf. The study was originally intended to mark out the differences in views of aging by looking at the East/West divide. The study intended to ask this question: Did the Eastern/Asian influence of Confucius's "filial piety" and the "practice of ancestor worship . . . promote positive views of aging and high esteem for older adults"? In contrast, would the Western

approach that oriented itself toward youth have a less positive view of aging? The researchers' neat and tidy hypothesis, however, turned out to be a little too tidy. It didn't leave room for the distinctiveness between Asian countries, etc.

13. Hubert Humphrey, quoted in Joe Hanson, "The Moral Test of Government," *HuffPost*, September 3, 2012, https://tinyurl.com/y79xlpeh.
14. Alessandra Malito, "Older Americans Are Sicker and Poorer Than Seniors in Other Wealthy Countries," MarketWatch, November 16, 2017, https://tinyurl.com/smh69wc.
15. Ignatius Charles Brady, Lawrence Cunningham, and the Editors of Encyclopaedia Britannica, "St. Francis of Assisi," *Encyclopaedia Britannica*, last updated December 2, 2019, https://tinyurl.com/wnhr2z7.
16. The Community of St. Francis, American Province, *The Canticle* 32, no. 2 (October 2014): 1, https://tinyurl.com/tq2dnhg.

Chapter 3: The Horror of the Body

1. Tom Hopkins, "Memento Mori: Death and Hell in Medieval Art," *Worchester Cathedral Library and Archive* (blog), June 3, 2015, https://tinyurl.com/w4fk599.
2. Ella Morton, "What Rot: A Look at the Striking 'Transi' Corpse Sculptures," *Atlas Obscura*, Slate, September 24, 2014, https://tinyurl.com/rc8q83a.
3. Cummins, "Attitudes to Old Age and Ageing,"

160.

4. Cummins, 160.
5. Cummins, 160–61.
6. Cummins, 161.
7. Alissa Wilkinson, "Midsommar Is a Brutish, Nasty, Daylight Nightmare from the Director of Hereditary," Vox, June 20, 2019, https://tinyurl.com/r5mjemh.
8. Cynthia Hahn, "Relics and Reliquaries: A Matter of Life and Death," lecture for Harn Eminent Scholar Chair in Art History Lecture Series (University of Florida's Harn Museum of Art: Gainesville, FL, March 16, 2017), video shared by UF Center for Humanities and the Public Sphere, January 9, 2019, 17:13, https://tinyurl.com/wnhx5tk.
9. For a good laugh and an informative take on incorruptible saints, see Caitlin Doughty, "How to Tell if Your Saint Is Incorrupt," November 5, 2015 in *Ask a Mortician*, YouTube video, https://tinyurl.com/tkwnh5x; mortician Caitlin Doughty is the author of *From Here to Eternity; Traveling the World to Find the Good Death.*
10. Thomas of Celano, *First Life* (London: Society for Promoting Christian Knowledge, 2000), 10.
11. Thomas of Celano, *First Life*, quoted in Jon M. Sweeney, *The Enthusiast: How the Best Friend of Francis of Assisi Almost Destroyed What He Started* (Notre Dame: Ave Maria Press, 2016), 13.
12. Sweeney, *The Enthusiast*, 15–16.
13. Emling, *Setting the World on Fire*, 6–7.
14. Emling, 202.

15. Emling, 202–4.
16. Emling, 205.
17. Christine Bednarz, "Bones of 30,000 Plague Victims Decorate This Church," *National Geographic*, October 26, 2017, https://tinyurl.com/yy66h5rj.
18. Hahn, "Relics and Reliquaries," 14.
19. Barbara Drake Boehm, "Relics and Reliquaries in Medieval Christianity," The Metropolitan Museum of Art (website), October 2001, https://tinyurl.com/rxh2n5k.
20. Caroline Walker Bynum and Paula Gerson, "Body-Part Reliquaries and Body Parts in the Middle Ages," *Gesta* 36, no. 1 (1997): 5, https://tinyurl.com/sszqqvy.
21. Hahn, "Relics and Reliquaries," 12:55.
22. Hahn.
23. Cummins, "Attitudes to Old Age and Ageing," 153.
24. Cummins, 154.

Chapter 4: Acts of Love

1. Originally published in a slightly different form in Christiana Peterson, "Wounds," *Good Letters*, January 9, 2019, https://tinyurl.com/sv4dbep.

Chapter 5: A Living Death

1. Veronica Mary Rolf, *An Explorer's Guide to Julian of Norwich* (Downers Grove, IL: IVP, 2018), 50.
2. Julian of Norwich, *Revelations of Divine Love*, in

Bernard McGinn, ed., *The Essential Writings of Christian Mysticism* (New York: The Modern Library, 2006), 243.

3. Elizabeth MacDonald, *Skirting Heresy: The Life and Times of Margery Kempe* (Cincinnati: Franciscan Media, 2014), 99.
4. MacDonald, 99.
5. Originally published in a slightly different form in Christiana Peterson, "The Anchoress Stares at Her Grave," *Good Letters*, July 31, 2019, https://tinyurl.com/tvgfsv8.

CHAPTER 6: THE SCORCHES OF PREDESTINATION

1. "Heinz Gaugel," Meet the Artist, Amish & Mennonite Heritage Center, accessed April 24, 2020, https://tinyurl.com/y7g2ltqo.
2. Ursula King, *Christian Mystics: Their Lives and Legacies throughout the Ages* (Mahwah, NJ: HiddenSpring, 2001), 91.
3. Editors of Encyclopaedia Britannica, s.v. "Black Death."
4. The Mennonite Quarterly Review, "Compassion for the Enemy," Goshen College, https://tinyurl.com/soohs32.
5. New World Encyclopedia contributors, s.v. "Humanism," New World Encyclopedia, last revised January 19, 2018, https://tinyurl.com/swqctvx.
6. Spinrad, *The Summons of Death*, 37.

7. Spinrad, 28.
8. Spinrad, 37.
9. Spinrad, 17.
10. Spinrad, 23.
11. Spinrad, 23.
12. Spinrad, 23.
13. Virginia Hughes, "When Do Kids Understand Death?," *National Geographic*, July 26, 2013, https://tinyurl.com/rplkw98.
14. Caitlin S. M. Cowan, Shui F. Wong, and Lillian Le, "Rethinking the Role of Thought Suppression in Psychological Models and Treatment," *Journal of Neuroscience* 37, no. 47 (November 2017): 11293–95, https://tinyurl.com/wl78zdr.
15. Spinrad, *The Summons of Death*, 47.
16. Spinrad, 48.
17. Spinrad, 49.
18. I've taken a little literary license with this story of Saint Francis de Sales. The story of his fear of hell and his mystical experience is true, but I've added some details in order to evoke the feeling of a panic attack.
19. This version of the Memorare is from "The Memorare," EWTN (website), https://tinyurl.com/y292zztn.
20. Saint Francis de Sales, *Consoling Thoughts on Sickness and Death*, comp. Père Huguet (Charlotte, NC: TAN Books, 2013), 60.
21. De Sales, 63.
22. Père Huguet, introduction to *Consoling Thoughts*, by de Sales, xviii.
23. Herbert Lockyer, *Psalms: A Devotional Commen-*

tary (Grand Rapids, MI: Kregel, 1993), 160.

24. Lockyer, 299.

CHAPTER 7: WOUNDS OF RESURRECTION

1. Originally published in a slightly different form in Christiana Peterson, "My Grandmother, Oneta—A Woman of Valor," *Rachel Held Evans* (blog), November 3, 2012, https://tinyurl.com/qvt6bqt.
2. Originally published in a slightly different form in Christiana Peterson, "The Wounds of Resurrection," *Good Letters*, April 19, 2016, https://tinyurl.com/y4yp2zm9.
3. "Caravaggio Biography," Caravaggio.org, https://tinyurl.com/uzh368c.
4. Desmond Seward, *Caravaggio: A Passionate Life* (London: Thistle Publishing, 2013), chap. 16, https://tinyurl.com/r7yjj7e.
5. Seward, chap. 16.
6. Pamela Askew, *Caravaggio's Death of the Virgin* (Princeton: Princeton University Press, 1990), 132, quoted in Seward, chap. 16.
7. Henri Nouwen, *Bread for the Journey: A Daybook of Wisdom and Faith* (New York: HarperOne, 2006), 26.
8. N. T. Wright, *Following Jesus: Biblical Reflections on Discipleship* (Grand Rapids, MI: Eerdmans, 2014), 107.

CHAPTER 8: LESSER DEATHS

1. King, *Christian Mystics*, 150.
2. McGinn, *Christian Mysticism*, 110.
3. Teresa of Ávila, *The Autobiography of St. Teresa of Avila*, trans. Kieran Kavanaugh and Otilio Rodriguez (New York: Book-of-the-Month Club, 1995), 251.
4. Teresa of Ávila, *Life*, quoted in McGinn, *Christian Mysticism*, 358.
5. Teresa, quoted in McGinn, 359.
6. Teresa, quoted in McGinn, 358.
7. Saint Teresa of Ávila, *The Interior Castle*, 3rd ed., trans. the Benedictines of Stanbrook, ed. Rev. Fr. Benedict Zimmerman (London: Thomas Baker, 1921), chap. 7, https://tinyurl.com/r8aggd4.
8. Saint Francis de Sales, quoted in Saint Alphonsus Liguori, *Meditations on the Passion of Our Lord* (Colorado Springs: The Seraphim Company, 2016), chap. 1, https://tinyurl.com/sayy39a.
9. Liguori, chap. 1.
10. Saint Francis de Sales, quoted in Liguori, chap. 2, https://tinyurl.com/sf4884r.
11. De Sales, *Consoling Thoughts*, 91.
12. Luke Timothy Johnson, *Hebrews: A Commentary* (Louisville: Westminster John Knox, 2006), 101. Johnson says that the author of Hebrews understood that this fear of death "supports and structures the patterns of compulsion that can be regarded as idolatry."
13. De Sales, *Consoling Thoughts*, 65.

14. Iserson, *Death to Dust*, 216.

CHAPTER 9: THE ODD VICTORIANS

1. Dennis Rasmussen, *The Infidel and the Professor: David Hume, Adam Smith, and the Friendship that Shaped Modern Thought* (Princeton, NJ: Princeton University Press, 2017), 1, quoted in Marina Benjamin, ed., "He Died as He Lived: David Hume, Philosopher and Infidel," Aeon, October 23, 2017, https://tinyurl.com/ybdg2teq. Reproduced under Creative Commons License CC BY-ND 4.0.
2. Schillace, *Death's Summer Coat*, 90.
3. Schillace, 90–91.
4. Schillace, 91.
5. Schillace, 90.
6. Charles Taylor talks about this in this article *Buffered and Porous Selves* in The Immanent Frame, September 2, 2008, https://tif.ssrc.org/2008/09/02/buffered-and-porous-selves.
7. Jill Lepore, "The Strange and Twisted Life of 'Frankenstein,'" *New Yorker*, February 5, 2018, https://tinyurl.com/ycl6vpae.
8. Sharon Ruston, "The Science of Life and Death in Mary Shelley's *Frankenstein*," British Library, May 15, 2014, https://tinyurl.com/y4l766pc.
9. Piers D. Mitchell et al., "The Study of Anatomy in England from 1700 to the Early 20th Century," *Journal of Anatomy* 219, no. 2 (August 2011): 91–99, https://tinyurl.com/upcm43u.
10. Schillace, *Death's Summer Coat*, 140.

11. George K. Behlmer, "Grave Doubts: Victorian Medicine, Moral Panic, and the Signs of Death," *Journal of British Studies* 42, no. 2 (April 2003): 217, https://tinyurl.com/t583gv2.
12. Schillace, *Death's Summer Coat*, 109–110.
13. Schillace, 116.
14. Chris Woodyard, ed., *The Victorian Book of the Dead* (Dayton, OH: Kestrel Publications, 2014), 253–54.
15. Schillace, *Death's Summer Coat*, 117.
16. Schillace, 117.

Chapter 10: An Artistic Sense for Death

1. William Raeper, *George MacDonald* (Oxford: Lion, 1987), 16.
2. Raeper, *George MacDonald*, 16.
3. Kirstin Jeffrey Johnson, "Rooted Deep: Relational Inkings of the Mythopoeic Maker, George MacDonald," in *Informing the Inklings: George MacDonald and the Victorian Roots of Modern Fantasy*, ed. Michael Partridge and Kirstin Jeffrey Johnson (Hamden, CT: Winged Lion Press, 2018), 34.
4. Stephen Prickett, "The Two Worlds of George MacDonald," *North Wind: A Journal of George MacDonald Studies* 2 (1983): 16, https://tinyurl.com/vfr8vew.
5. Raeper, *George MacDonald*, 107.
6. Friedrich Schlegel, quoted in Raeper, *George*

MacDonald, 107.

7. Raeper, *George MacDonald*, 107.
8. Daniel Gabelman, "Organised Innocence: MacDonald, Lewis and Literature 'For the Childlike,'" in *Informing the Inklings*, 78–79.

CHAPTER 11: UNLOCKING THE IMPRISONED MIND

1. Malcolm Guite, "'Needles of Eternal Light': How Coleridge Aroused MacDonald and Lewis," in *Informing the Inklings*, 27.
2. George MacDonald, "The Golden Key," in *The Heart of George MacDonald: A One-Volume Collection of His Most Important Fiction, Essays, Sermons, Drama, Poetry, Letters*, ed. Rolland Hein (Vancouver: Regent College, 2004), 202.
3. MacDonald, "The Golden Key," 211.
4. Rolland Hein, *Christian Mythmakers* (Chicago: Cornerstone Press, 2002), 92.
5. Kirstin Jeffrey Johnson and Jennifer Trafton, "Giving as the Angels Give: The Imaginative Hospitality of George MacDonald" (presentation, Hutchmoot conference, Nashville, TN, October 12, 2019).
6. Johnson and Trafton.
7. Johnson and Trafton.
8. MacDonald, *A Book of Strife in the Form of the Diary of an Old Soul*, "January 4," in *The Heart of George MacDonald*, 217.
9. MacDonald, *A Book of Strife in the Form of the*

Diary of an Old Soul, "February 23," in *The Heart of George MacDonald*, 219.

10. MacDonald to Eva Pym, Vancouver, 28 September 1889, in *The Heart of George MacDonald*, 11.
11. MacDonald to Adelaide Pym, Vancouver, 8 February 1890, in *The Heart of George MacDonald*, 12.
12. MacDonald to Adelaide Pym, Vancouver, 8 February 1890, in *The Heart of George MacDonald*, 13.
13. Hein, *Christian Mythmakers*, 66.

CHAPTER 12: THE COURAGE OF FAIRY

1. Madeleine L'Engle, *Walking on Water: Reflections on Faith and Art* (Colorado Springs: Waterbrook Press, 2001), 3.
2. Donna E. Norton, *Through the Eyes of a Child: An Introduction to Children's Literature*, 5th ed. (Columbus, OH: Merrill, 1999), 63.
3. Gabelman, "Organised Innocence," 72.
4. Gabelman, 73.
5. Gabelman, 74.
6. Gabelman, 75.
7. Kimberley Reynolds, "Perceptions of Childhood," British Library, May 15, 2014, https://tinyurl.com/y76j6cab.
8. Gabelman, "Organised Innocence," 77.
9. Lewis Carroll, "The Letters of Lewis Carroll," quoted in Gabelman, 76.
10. Gabelman, 76.

11. Gabelman, 77.
12. George MacDonald. Originally printed as the preface to an American edition to *The Light Princess and Other Fairy Tales* in 1893, the essay was then included in *A Dish of Orts*, quoted in Raeper, *George MacDonald*, 306.
13. L'Engle, *Walking on Water*, 226.
14. Amy Peterson, *Where Goodness Still Grows: Reclaiming Virtue in an Age of Hypocrisy* (Nashville: W Publishing Group, 2020), xxii.
15. Robert Coles, *The Spiritual Life of Children* (Houghton Mifflin: Boston, 1990), p. 37, quoted in Vigen Guroian, *Tending the Heart of Virtue: How Classic Stories Awaken a Child's Moral Imagination* (New York: Oxford University Press, 1998), 63.
16. Gabelman, "Organised Innocence," 79.
17. Gabelman, 87.
18. L'Engle, *Walking on Water*, 186.

CHAPTER 13: FALLING FROM A DINOSAUR

1. Originally published in a slightly different form in Christiana Peterson, "How Farm Life Taught Our Kids About Death," *Christianity Today*, May 8, 2014, https://tinyurl.com/t7yre5b.
2. Richard Beck, *The Slavery of Death* (Eugene, OR: Cascade, 2014), 28.
3. Beck, 29.
4. Beck, 28.

5. Hanna Rosin, "The Overprotected Kid," *Atlantic*, April 2014, https://tinyurl.com/humjuyx.
6. Amy Morin, "10 Reasons Teens Have So Much Anxiety Today," *Psychology Today*, November 3, 2017, https://tinyurl.com/wfhuz9t.
7. Rosin, "The Overprotected Kid."
8. D. L. Mayfield, "Church Planting and the Gospel of Gentrification," *Sojourners*, July 2017, https://tinyurl.com/vpnzeye.
9. Christopher Ingraham, "There's Never Been a Safer Time to Be a Kid in America," *Washington Post*, April 14, 2015, https://tinyurl.com/ufetd3e.
10. Lindsay Moore, "Police, Survivors Debunk Human Trafficking Kidnapping Myths," MLive, January 16, 2020, https://tinyurl.com/rn9n5u9.
11. Jack Healy, "In Indian Country, a Crisis of Missing Women. And a New One When They're Found," *New York Times*, December 25, 2019, https://tinyurl.com/wk8h728.
12. Lara Powers, "Op-Ed: Why a Mom's Facebook Warning about Human Traffickers Hurts Sex-Trafficked Kids," *Los Angeles Times*, April 3, 2017, https://tinyurl.com/ulsyhk9.
13. Moore, "Police, Survivors Debunk Human Trafficking."

CHAPTER 14: THE COMMUNAL RITUALS OF DEATH

1. Originally published in a slightly different form in Christiana Peterson, "Doorways to Death," *Good Letters*, August 20, 2018, https://tinyurl.com/ryox6kg.
2. Iserson, *Death to Dust*, 452.
3. Saint Jerome, *Vita Pauli*, quoted in Iserson, 451.
4. Iserson, *Death to Dust*, 448.
5. Iserson, 24–25.
6. Iserson, 424.
7. Iserson, 425.
8. Jessica Mitford, *The American Way of Death Revisited* (New York: Knopf Doubleday Publishing Group, 2011), 14.
9. "How Much Does a Funeral Cost?," Lincoln Heritage Funeral Advantage, https://tinyurl.com/y4ce55st.
10. Mark Harris, *Grave Matters: A Journey Through the Modern Funeral Industry to a Natural Way of Burial* (New York: Scribner, 2007), 29.
11. Iserson, *Death to Dust*, 193.
12. Harris, *Grave Matters*, 45.
13. Iserson, *Death to Dust*, 225.
14. Traci Rylands, "The Strange Case of Dr. Thomas Holmes," *Adventures in Cemetery Hopping*, June 7, 2013, https://tinyurl.com/t2aztmg.
15. Harris, *Grave Matters*, 42–45.
16. Iserson, *Death to Dust*, 195.
17. Rylands, "The Strange Case of Dr. Thomas

Holmes."

18. Harris, *Grave Matters*, 110.
19. Thurman, *The Negro Spiritual Speaks of Life and Death*, 19.
20. Thurman, 19.

Chapter 15: The Tensions of Death and Life

1. Howard Zinn, *A People's History of the United States*, deluxe ed. (New York: Harper Perennial, 2010), 49.
2. Zinn, 29.
3. Jamelle Bouie, "The Enlightenment's Dark Side," Slate, June 5, 2018, https://tinyurl.com/y8lzrunk.
4. David Bindman, "Blake's Vision of Slavery Revisited," *Huntington Library Quarterly* 58, no. 3/4 (1995): 373, https://tinyurl.com/rod33pv.
5. William Blake, "The Little Black Boy," Poetry Foundation, https://tinyurl.com/ydaadgbq.
6. Bindman, "Blake's Vision of Slavery Revised,"382.
7. W. Terry Whalin, *Sojourner Truth: American Abolitionist* (Uhrichsville, OH: Barbour Publishing, 1997), 9.
8. Sojourner Truth, *The Narrative of Sojourner Truth*, ed. Olive Gilbert (Boston: self-pub., 1850), chap. 2, https://tinyurl.com/wjhogb7.
9. Truth, chap. 3, https://tinyurl.com/tqcttej.
10. Truth, chap. 4, https://tinyurl.com/uzbolk2.

11. Truth, chap. 3.
12. Truth, chap. 4.
13. Truth, chap. 19, https://tinyurl.com/rohqqv7.
14. Truth, chap. 9, https://tinyurl.com/tol3c5w.
15. Truth, chap. 12, https://tinyurl.com/upx4g4f.
16. Truth, chap. 13, https://tinyurl.com/spe2uyq.
17. John W. Blassingame, ed., *Slave Testimony: Two Centuries of Letters, Speeches, Interviews, and Autobiographies* (Baton Rouge and London: Louisiana State University Press, 1977), 541, quoted in M. Shawn Copeland, *Knowing Christ Crucified: The Witness of African American Religious Experience* (New York: Orbis Books, 2018), 25.
18. Copeland, 25.
19. Truth, *The Narrative of Sojourner Truth*, chap. 15, https://tinyurl.com/unanck8.
20. Truth, chap. 19.
21. "On This Day—May 29, 1851: Sojourner Truth Addresses Ohio Women's Rights Convention; Record of Speech Later Rewritten by White Feminist," A History of Racial Injustice Calendar, Equal Justice Initiative, https://tinyurl.com/rk4mnge.
22. Nick Buckley, "The 'Ain't I a Woman' Speech Made Sojourner Truth Famous. The Version You Know Isn't What She Said," *Battle Creek Enquirer*, March 1, 2020, https://tinyurl.com/yd48ffbu.
23. "The Readings," The Sojourner Truth Project, https://tinyurl.com/tgx2o3k.
24. Rev. Marius Robinson, "Women's Rights Con-

vention," *Anti-Slavery Bugle*, June 21, 1851, https://tinyurl.com/uohnf3e.

25. "Sojourner Truth Addresses Ohio Women's Rights Convention."
26. Achille Mbembe, "Necropolitics," trans. Libby Meintjes, *Public Culture* 15, no. 1 (Winter 2003): 21, quoted in Copeland, *Knowing Christ Crucified*, 85.
27. Thurman, "The Negro Spiritual Speaks of Life and Death," 14, 15.
28. Copeland, *Knowing Christ Crucified*, 32.
29. Cox, *A Handbook of Christian Mysticism*, 34.
30. Denise Fidia, "'That Ain't Anything but a Way to Say Something': Apophatic Unsaying in *Wise Blood*," *Flannery O'Connor Review* 5 (2007): 119, https://tinyurl.com/vbvjm48.
31. Cox, *A Handbook of Christian Mysticism*, 113.
32. Cox, 112.
33. Copeland, *Knowing Christ Crucified*, 34.
34. Copeland, 35.
35. "African American Spirituals," Library of Congress, https://tinyurl.com/yblyb6f6.
36. Thurman, *The Negro Spiritual Speaks of Life and Death*, 15.
37. Thurman, 20.
38. Thurman, 24.
39. Thurman, 24.
40. Thurman, 37.
41. Copeland, *Knowing Christ Crucified*, 33–34.
42. Thurman, *The Negro Spiritual Speaks of Life and Death*, 38.
43. Thurman, 30.

44. Thurman, 30.
45. Adam Serwer, "The Myth of the Kindly General Lee," *Atlantic*, June 2017, https://tinyurl.com/yafjaq5a.
46. Roy Blount, Jr. "Making Sense of Robert E. Lee," *Smithsonian*, July 2003, https://tinyurl.com/yb6kcwwu.
47. Talibah Chiku, "For We Are One," Ernest Becker Foundation, July 16, 2019, https://tinyurl.com/us96v2k.

CHAPTER 16: BETWEEN BIRTH AND DEATH

1. Rachel Marie Stone, *Birthing Hope: Giving Fear to the Light* (Downers Grove, IL: InterVarsity Press, 2018), 53.
2. Stone, 55.
3. Bethany Sollereder, "Episode 54: 'Death Is a Very Good Part of Life,'" interview by Joe Davis, October 27, 2018, in *Mid-Faith Crisis*, published by Nick Page, podcast, MP4 audio, 16:11, https://tinyurl.com/ursh4g4.
4. "Evasion of Apoptosis: A Hallmark of Cancer," Genetech, https://tinyurl.com/rsqosur.
5. Nina Martin and Renee Montagne, "U.S. Has the Worst Rate of Maternal Deaths in the Developed World," NPR, May 12, 2017, https://tinyurl.com/yccnpp6s.
6. Mary Beth Flanders-Stepans, "Alarming Racial Differences in Maternal Mortality," *Journal of*

Perinatal Education 9, no. 2 (Spring 2000): 50–51, https://tinyurl.com/ya7cp24b.

7. Amy Roeder, "America Is Failing Its Black Mothers," *Harvard Public Health*, Winter 2019, https://tinyurl.com/yb7gb5wf.
8. Maya Salam, "For Serena Williams, Childbirth Was a Harrowing Ordeal. She's Not Alone.," *New York Times*, January 11, 2018, https://tinyurl.com/ybm2ud5k.
9. Roeder, "America Is Failing Its Black Mothers."
10. Originally published in a slightly different form in Christiana N. Peterson, "Midwifing Pain: A Book Review of Birthing Hope," *Bearings Online*, June 28, 2018, https://tinyurl.com/w3gzzdq.

CHAPTER 17: CONQUERING NATURE

1. Brian Roewe, "Francis: Caring for the Earth a Thank-You Note to God," *Eco Catholic*, May 22, 2014, https://tinyurl.com/srhgque.
2. Randy S. Woodley, *Living in Color: Embracing God's Passion for Ethnic Diversity* (Downers Grove, IL: InterVarsity, 2001), 48–49, quoted in Randy S. Woodley, *Shalom and the Community of Creation: An Indigenous Vision* (Grand Rapids: Eerdmans, 2012), 98.
3. Woodley, *Shalom and the Community of Creation*, 101.
4. Woodley, 102.
5. "Sources of Greenhouse Gas Emissions," United States Environmental Protection

Agency, https://tinyurl.com/uj4svwe.

6. Coral Davenport, "The Marshall Islands Are Disappearing," *New York Times*, December 2, 2015, https://tinyurl.com/jjeoeuv.
7. Tim McDonnell, "The Refugees the World Barely Pays Attention To," NPR, June 20, 2018, https://tinyurl.com/y9d7nvze.
8. A term coined by Essam El-Hinnawi that describes "people who have been forced to leave their traditional habitat, temporarily or permanently, because of a marked environmental disruption (natural and/or triggered by people) that jeopardizes their existence and/or seriously affects the quality of their life." https://tinyurl.com/yce9k7q5.
9. A. J. Swoboda, *Subversive Sabbath: The Surprising Power of Rest in a Nonstop World* (Grand Rapids: Brazos Press, 2018), 126.
10. Davenport, "The Marshall Islands Are Disappearing."
11. John D. Sutter, "You're Making This Island Disappear," CNN, June 2015, https://tinyurl.com/y27t2tzz.
12. Ernest Becker, *Escape from Evil* (New York: Free Press, 1975), 72, quoted in "We Are Ruining the Theatre of Our Immortality: Death Denial & Climate Change," Ernest Becker Foundation, https://tinyurl.com/rfuy7we.
13. "Death Denial & Climate Change."
14. Carl McColman, *Christian Mystics: 108 Seers, Saints, and Sages* (Charlottesville, VA: Hampton Roads Publishing, 2016), 105.

15. Thomas Cahill, "First Chapter: 'Mysteries of the Middle Ages,'" *New York Times*, December 24, 2006, https://tinyurl.com/ttwtngw.
16. Frances M. Malpezzi, "Evergreen: The Enduring Voice of a Nine-Hundred-Year-Old Healer," in *Healing Logics: Culture and Medicine in Modern Health Belief Systems*, ed. Erika Brady (Logan, UT: University Press of Colorado, 2001), 165, https://tinyurl.com/sczcd92.
17. Malpezzi, 169.
18. Malpezzi, 170.
19. Malpezzi, 170.
20. Matthew Fox, *Illuminations of Hildegard of Bingen* (Santa Fe: Bear, 1985), 8, quoted in Malpezzi, "Evergreen," 172.
21. Malpezzi, "Evergreen," 172.
22. Woodley, *Shalom and the Community of Creation*, 67.
23. Woodley, 68.
24. Beck, *The Slavery of Death*, 3.
25. Ernest Becker, *The Denial of Death* (1973; repr., New York: Free Press Paperbacks, 1997), xvii. All subsequent citations refer to this edition.
26. Becker, xiii.
27. Sam Keen, foreword to Becker, *The Denial of Death*, xiii–xiv.
28. Keen, foreword to Becker, xiii.
29. Keen, foreword to Becker, xiv.
30. Jack Martin and Daniel Liechty, "Ernest Becker's Dark Turn (1971–1973)," *Journal of Humanistic Psychology* 29, no. 2 (October 2016): 10, https://doi.org/10.1177/0022167816671580.

CHAPTER 18: A LONELY DEATH

1. Originally published in a slightly different form in Christiana N. Peterson, "The Lost Goodbye," *Good Letters*, October 3, 2018, https://tinyurl.com/s47mf7b.
2. Norimitsu Onishi, "A Generation in Japan Faces a Lonely Death," *New York Times*, November 30, 2017, https://tinyurl.com/yctnjohb.
3. Onishi, "Lonely Death."
4. Onishi, "Lonely Death."
5. "America's Suicide Rate Has Increased for 13 Years in a Row," *Economist*, January 30, 2020, https://tinyurl.com/v46l42a.
6. Arthur C. Brooks, "How Loneliness Is Tearing America Apart," *New York Times*, November 23, 2018, https://tinyurl.com/y8dp8hso.
7. "Why Become a Doula," International End of Life Doula Association, https://tinyurl.com/ww3vnqb.
8. Danae King, "Death Doulas Provide Support, Comfort and a New Option for the Dying and Their Families," *USA Today*, December 3, 2019, https://tinyurl.com/uw3g4nz.

CHAPTER 19: GRIEF

1. I write about this in my book *Mystics and Misfits: Meeting God Through St. Francis and Other Unlikely Saints* (Harrisonburg, VA: Herald Press, 2018).
2. Tova Gamliel, "Tears and Ideas: Therapeutic

Aspects of 'Traditional' Wailing Performance," *Journal of Ritual Studies* 28, no. 1 (2014): 46, https://tinyurl.com/rnqlm9u.

3. Gamliel, 47. Brackets in the original.
4. Alan D. Wolfelt, "The Journey through Grief: The Six Needs of Mourning," Center for Loss & Life Transition, December 14, 2016, https://tinyurl.com/uesnhwe.
5. Helaine Selin and Robert M. Rakoff, eds., *Death across Cultures: Death and Dying in Non-Western Cultures*, Science across Cultures: The History of Non-Western Science (Cham, Switzerland: Springer, 2019), 110.
6. William L. Hamilton, "A Consolation of Voices: At the Park Avenue Armory, Mourning the World Over," *New York Times*, September 11, 2016, https://tinyurl.com/wtae63w.
7. Hamilton, "A Consolation of Voices."
8. Hamilton, "A Consolation of Voices."
9. Kathleen M. O'Connor, *Lamentations and the Tears of the World* (New York: Orbis Books, 2002), 3.
10. Gamliel, "Tears and Ideas," 45.
11. O'Connor, *Lamentations and the Tears of the World*, 4.

Chapter 20: A Good Death

1. Paul Kalanithi, *When Breath Becomes Air* (New York: Random House, 2016), 199.
2. Kalanithi, 219.
3. Sarah H. Cross and Haider J. Warraich, "More

Americans Are Dying at Home. Is That a Good Thing?," STAT, December 11, 2019, https://tinyurl.com/ucs2b4v.

4. Ann Neumann, *The Good Death: An Exploration of Dying in America* (Boston: Beacon Press, 2016), 27.
5. Neumann, 26.
6. Cross and Warraich, "More Americans Are Dying at Home."
7. Keen, foreword to Becker, *The Denial of Death*, xv.
8. Keen, foreword to Becker, xiv.
9. Keen, foreword to Becker, xiv–xv.

Chapter 21: The Spiritual Practice of Dying

1. "How Death Came to Dinner," Death Over Dinner, https://tinyurl.com/srj48jl.
2. *Parks and Recreation*, season 5, episode 7, "Leslie vs. April," directed by Wendey Stanzler, written by Harris Wittels, aired November 15, 2012, on NBC.
3. Jonathan Jong, "Faith and the Fear of Death," *The New Atlantis*, no. 55 (Spring 2018): 94, https://tinyurl.com/sl6j6sz.
4. John Romanides, *TheAncestral Sin* (Ridgewood, NJ: Zephyr, 2002), 116, quoted in Beck, *The Slavery of Death*, 24.
5. Beck, 24.

CONCLUSION: ANOINTING THE GRAVE

1. Shawn Langlois, "One journalist's 'brilliant' take on the coronavirus pandemic cheered as 'the best cold open . . . to a news show'," MarketWatch, April 9, 2020, https://tinyurl.com/yak4wsdz.
2. Joan Chittister, *Between the Dark and the Daylight: Embracing the Contradictions of Life* (New York: Image, 2015), 11.
3. Saint Bonaventure, "Prayer in Darkness & Silence," in "Mystical Prayer in the Holy Spirit—Bonaventure," Crossroads Initiative, July 15, 2019, https://tinyurl.com/tdqfpjv.

TIMELINE

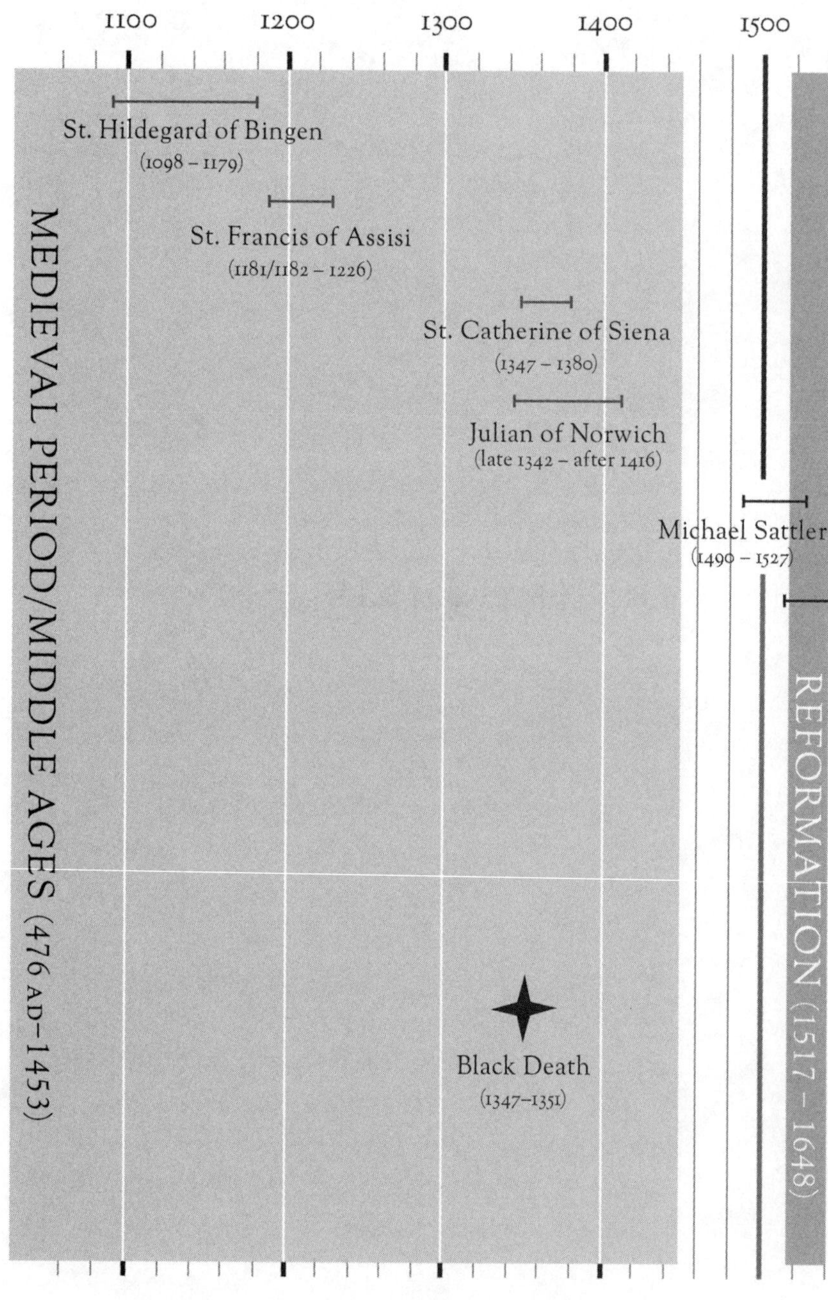

1100
1200
1300
1400
1500
St. Hildegard of Bingen
(1098 – 1179)
St. Francis of Assisi
(1181/1182 – 1226)
St. Catherine of Siena
(1347 – 1380)
Julian of Norwich
(late 1342 – after 1416)
Michael Sattler
(1490 – 1527)
Medieval Period/Middle Ages (476 AD–1453)
Reformation (1517 – 1648)
Black Death
(1347–1351)

TIMELINE

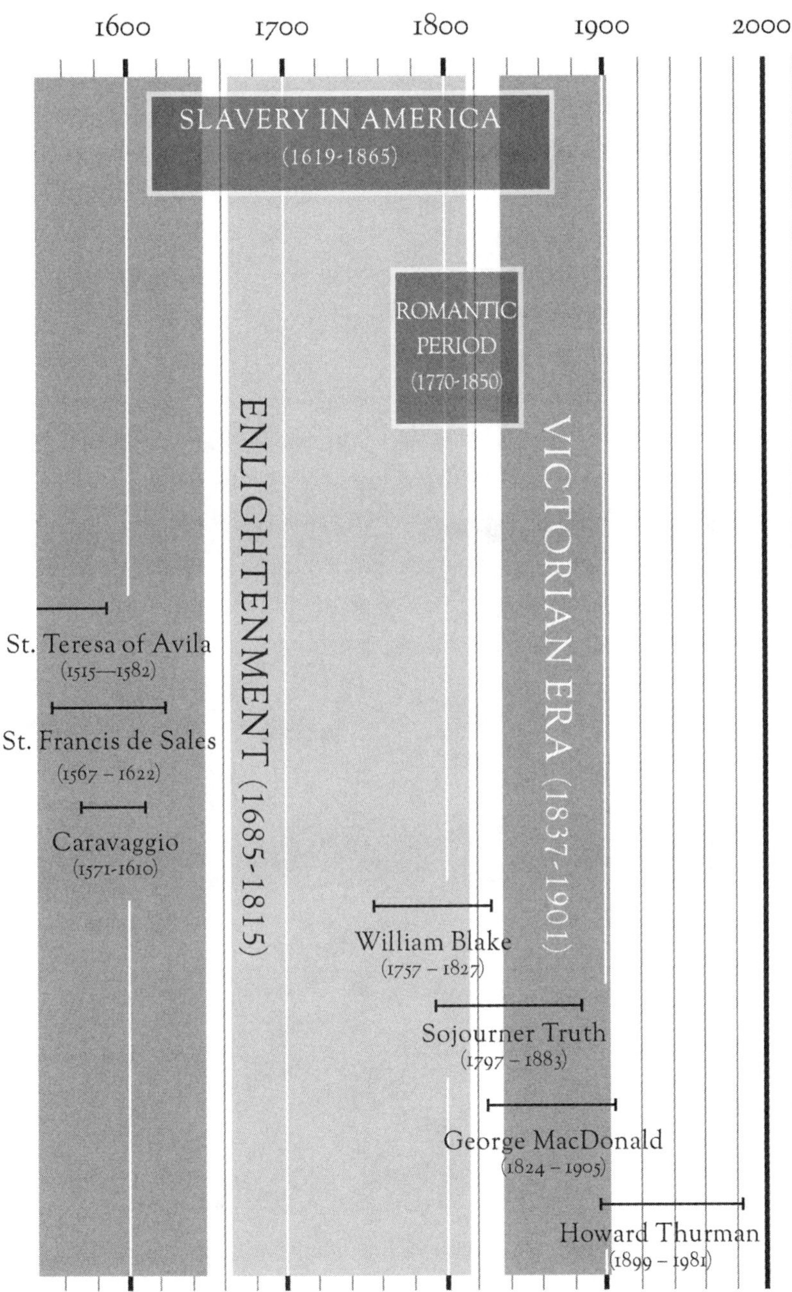
1600
1700
1800
1900
2000
SLAVERY IN AMERICA
(1619-1865)
ROMANTIC
PERIOD
(1770-1850)
ENLIGHTENMENT (1685-1815)
VICTORIAN ERA (1837-1901)
St. Teresa of Avila
(1515—1582)
St. Francis de Sales
(1567 – 1622)
Caravaggio
(1571-1610)
William Blake
(1757 – 1827)
Sojourner Truth
(1797 – 1883)
George MacDonald
(1824 – 1905)
Howard Thurman
(1899 – 1981)